Footprint Handbook
Guyana, Guyane
& Suriname

BEN BOX

This is
the Guianas

Even though language and colonial legacies separate them, the Guianas share a landscape dominated by bronze-tinted rivers which flow from wildlife-rich forests and mountains to a populated coastal strip on the Atlantic Ocean.

Guyana's coast is a blend of coconut palms and Caribbean music, Dutch place names and drainage systems, Hindu temples, Islamic mosques and Demerara sugar. Georgetown, the capital, is known as the 'Garden City of the Caribbean', which gives some idea of the country's commercial and cultural orientation. In the thinly populated interior, life revolves around Amerindian communities beside the rivers, or, further south, the scattered ranches of the Rupununi Savannah. Waterfalls tumble over jasper rocks, or, at Kaieteur, into a chasm almost five times the height of Niagara.

Suriname, too, has been influenced by a variety of cultures, Amerindian, African, European and Asian. Markets, customs, festivals and food all reflect this. In Paramaribo, the capital, there is some fine Dutch colonial wooden architecture and there are important Jewish monuments. The Maroons, descendants of escaped slaves, have maintained traditional African culture for centuries and, together with the Amerindians, have a special bond with the tropical forest. Nature reserves include the combined parks of the Central Suriname Nature Reserve, Brownsberg, Wia-Wia and Galibi. The last two protect nesting ground for marine turtles.

Cayenne, the capital of Guyane, is on a peninsula at the mouth of the river of the same name. The department is known internationally for its space station at Kourou, from which over half the world's commercial satellites have been launched. An unusual attraction is the remains of the former penal colony, notably the Iles du Salut, made famous by Henri Charrière's book Papillon. Much of the country remains sparsely populated and two million hectares of the interior comprise the Parc Amazonien de Guyane which, with neighbouring reserves in Brazil, forms the world's largest protected tropical forest.

Ben Box

Best of
the Guianas

❶ Kaieteur Falls (Guyana)

Five times the height of Niagara and surrounded by unspoilt forest with many special natural features, the falls are a must. You can either take a tour with a flight to the plateau at the top, or trek in, which takes three or four days. Page 33.

❷ Iwokrama (Guyana)

A project for the conservation of primary tropical forest and study of sustainability where you can trek, take boat trips and stay in camps deep in the jungle. Two main lodges, Iwokrama itself and Atta, give unparalleled access to wildlife and Surama community is just outside. Page 34.

❸ Rupununi Savannah (Guyana)

This extensive grassland, which floods annually, has scattered Amerindian communities, is threaded with rivers and brims with birdlife. Giant anteaters, black caiman and giant river otters are also found here. Stay on ranches or in purpose-built lodges. Page 36.

❹ Paramaribo (Suriname)

A wonderful blend of European architecture and South American craft has led to UNESCO status for the beautiful historic centre. The city has a colourful market, a variety of cuisines, good nightlife and dolphin-watching trips where the Suriname and Commewijne rivers meet. Page 57.

❺ Sugar plantations in Commewijne (Suriname)

Within easy reach of Paramaribo are reminders of the days when sugar was the source of wealth for the colonists and cause of misery for their slaves. You can visit estates like Frederiksdorp and Peperpot, ruined sugar mills and lost plantations, now full of wildlife, which lead to turtle beaches on the Atlantic. Page 62.

❼ Kourou (Guyane)

The European space centre here is the big draw, with rocket launches a major spectacle, but fishing, bathing and other excursions as far as St-Laurent du Maroni are also on offer. Page 78.

❻ Central Suriname Nature Reserve (Suriname)

This immense protected area of pristine primary tropical forest teems with life. The most accessible part is the Raleighvallen/ Voltzberg Nature Reserve, a combination of dramatic rapids and a granite monolith rising above the dense jungle. Page 66.

❽ Iles du Salut (Guyane)

This group of former prison islands, brought to the attention of the world by its famous escapee, Henri Charrière, author of *Papillon*, is a popular hour's trip by boat from Kourou. They have now been reclaimed by nature, but if you wish to stay there is a hotel on Ile Royale. Page 79.

9 Kaw marshes (Guyane)

East of Roura are the swamps of Kaw, a great place to see unusual birds like hoatzin and scarlet ibis and three types of caiman. There are short boat excursions and longer stays on houseboats in the marshes. From Roura, too, there are boat trips inland and to island nature reserves off the coast. Pages 82.

Brokopondo Reservoir, Suriname

Route planner

A visit to the Guianas can be anything from a few days to a few weeks. Much depends on whether you intend to visit one, two or all three countries and how much travelling you plan to do independently. Outside the capitals, ranches and lodges are few and far between, giving privileged access to wildlife and local communities that you will not find elsewhere. Entrusting some of your trip to a reliable tour operator, who can arrange flights, road and river travel, can speed things up and provide good value.

Seven to ten days

capital cities, day trips and a lodge or two

In a week's visit you would be hard pressed to see more than one country, but seven to 10 days would give enough time to see some of the more important sites in Guyana, Suriname or Guyane. In each case you could spend a couple of nights in the capital. Both Georgetown and Paramaribo have more to see than Cayenne so in the last-named a night would suffice.

In Guyana and Suriname you can make day trips out of the capital. In Guyana, most are organized by operators, for instance to the Santa Mission area, birdwatching trips and days out to the Essequibo River. Also in Guyana there are day trips involving flights to the Kaieteur Falls, on its own or in combination with the Orinduik Falls or a resort. In Suriname, it is possible to make short excursions on public transport, although some bus routes may require an overnight stay. You can also rent a bicycle or take a cycle tour to Peperpot and other plantations in Commewijne district. Other popular day trips include Frederiksdorp Plantation (which is well set up for overnight stays), Jodensavane, Brownsberg (also with overnight possibilities) and boat tours near Paramaribo. In each country you should include in a short itinerary a three- to four-day trip to more distant destinations (or longer if you reduce time in and around the capital): lodges in the Rupununi or Iwokrama in Guyana; lodges on the Suriname River or to less accessible national parks like Galibi or Raleighvallen/Voltzberg.

Guyane lends itself well to a week to 10 days, with Kourou plus the Iles du Salut and the Roura and Kaw areas being two distinct destinations where you can spend two to three days each exploring different sites. The former can be visited independently, while the latter is best booked through an operator or floating hotel. If you hire a car you can easily visit the country's main places of interest, going as far as the borders with Suriname and Brazil on paved roads.

Two to three weeks
community tourism and trips into the wilds

An additional 10 to 14 days will allow for an extra night in Georgetown and Paramaribo to see more than just the city highlights. You would also be able to combine week-long visits to two or three countries. Bus transport from each capital to the border is quick (a bit too rapid for comfort in some instances), but crossing the rivers can be time-consuming with border formalities and limited ferry crossings, especially across the Corentyne River between Guyana and Suriname. You need to confirm crossings in advance. Flying between the countries is quicker, but you have to factor in the increased price, transfers and the airport hanging-about time.

More days will give far greater scope for special-interest tours, both natural and cultural, based around Amerindian or Maroon communities. In few cases can you reach the lodges or resorts concerned by public transport. A notable exception is Frederiksdorp in Suriname. In Guyana, the improvement of the road from Georgetown to Lethem on the Brazilian border, with a minibus service, opens up the interior for easier exploration. For instance, Iwokrama, Surama and Annai can be reached from this route, but this area remains largely untouched with many lodges reached by river, special road transfer from the lodge itself, or plane. With more time you can also build into the itinerary the four-day overland trek to Kaieteur, or other more adventurous trips. In Suriname, some of the furthest lodges from Paramaribo can only be reached by plane and an organized tour of four to eight days.

One month
take time to enjoy the interior to the full

On the basis of the above suggestions, the greater the length of your stay, the more flexibility there is for combining longer visits to each country, especially if travelling independently, extending the number of places you visit in the interior and adding some relaxation in what otherwise may be an energetic itinerary.

When to go

… and when not to

Climate

Although hot, the climate of the Guianas is not unhealthy. Throughout the region, mean shade temperature over the year is 27°C; the mean maximum is about 31°C and the mean minimum 23°C. Night and day temperatures vary more in the interior and highlands. The heat is tempered by cooling breezes from the sea, which are most appreciated in the warmest months, August to October. This period is, however, the best time to visit. There are minor variations in the wet seasons. In **Guyana** the rainy seasons are from May to June and from December to the end of January, although they may extend into the months either side. In the south and the Rupununi the wet season is May to July or August. Rainfall averages 2300 mm a year in Georgetown. In **Suriname**, average annual rainfall is about 2340 mm for Paramaribo and 1930 mm for the western division. The seasons are: small rainy season from November to February; small dry season from February to April; large rainy season from April to August; large dry season from August to November. Neither one of these seasons is, however, either very dry or very wet. The degree of cloudiness is fairly high and the average humidity is 82%. The climate of the interior is similar but with higher rainfall. In **Guyane**, the rainy season is November to July, sometimes with a dry period in February and March. The great rains begin in May.

Festivals

See also Public holidays, page 112.

Guyana

The **Republic Day** celebrations (23 February) last for one day, but there are other activities (children's costume competition, etc) which take place during the preceding days. **Mashramani** (Mash) is the Guyanese equivalent of carnival and coincides with Republic Day. There are float parades, calypso and soca music, dancing and other events. Also, in the two weeks prior to 23 February, many large companies hold Mashramani Camps at which public participation is encouraged. Hotels in Georgetown are very full, as they are also during international cricket matches. At Eastertime the main event in the **Rupununi**, the Rodeo at Lethem, is held. Around 21-28 August, **Jam Zone Summer Break** is held at the Guyana National Stadium and HJ Water World in Providence, East Bank Demerara (Facebook: JamzoneSummerBreak) with concerts, pageants, fashion shows and sporting events. Also in August is the **Bartica Regatta**. September is **Heritage month** for indigenous communities, with games, food and drink in each village. One community is selected each year as the central point for a joint festival.

Suriname

The main tourist seasons are 19 December to March and July and August. Mid-October to end-November is also popular.

Surifesta (http://surifesta.com) is a year-end festival, from mid-December to the second week of January, with shows, street parties and flower markets, culminating in a massive parade outside **'t Vat** and the igniting of giant strings of red *pagara* firecrackers in the centre of Paramaribo on 31 December. **Avondvierdaagse (Four-Day Walk)**, starting on the first Wednesday after Easter, is a carnival parade of the young and old dressed in traditional costumes or just simple outfits; it is organized by **BVVS-Fernandes** (Johannes Mungrastraat 5, Paramaribo, T475623, www.bvss.sr or see Facebook). At the **Suriname Jazz Festival** (www.jazzfestivalsuriname.com) local and international jazz musicians perform in Paramaribo; it is held annually in October. **Nationale Kunstbeurs/National Art Fair/National Art Exhibition**, is held at various locations in Paramaribo in October/November (see Facebook: nationalekunstbeurssuriname).

In early November the **Savanne Rally** attracts international drivers for a three-day, off-road rally in 4WDs in remote parts of the country. Some details in Dutch can be found on **www.sarkonline.com**, or see the **Surinaamse Auto Rally Klub** (SARK Facebook page).

Guyane

Guyane's Carnaval is joyous and interesting. It is principally a Créole event, but with some participation by all the different cultural groups in the department (best known are the contributions of the Brazilian and Haitian communities). Celebrations begin in January, with festivities every weekend, and culminate in colourful parades, music and dance during the four days preceding Ash Wednesday. Each day has its own motif and the costumes are very elaborate. On Saturday night, a dance called *Chez Nana – Au Soleil Levant* is held, for which the women disguise themselves beyond recognition as *Touloulous*, and ask the men to dance. They are not allowed to refuse. Since 1988 an additional dance has been added to Carnaval, *Le Bal Tololo*, on Friday night, the day before *Chez Nana*, in which the men disguise themselves with masks and fancy costumes and invite the women to dance. On Sunday there are parades in downtown Cayenne. There are also street parades in other places, like Kourou and St-Laurent du Maroni, usually earlier in the year than in Cayenne. **Lundi Gras** is the day to ridicule marriage, with mock wedding parties featuring men as brides and women as grooms. *Vaval*, the devil and soul of Carnaval, appears on **Mardi Gras** with dancers sporting red costumes, horns, tails, pitch-forks, etc. He is burnt that night (in the form of a straw doll) on a bonfire in the Place des Palmistes. **Ash Wednesday** is a time of sorrow, with participants dressed in black and white.

A full list of events can be found on **www.guyane-amazonie.fr**, but look out for the **Kali'na Amerindian Games** in early December, held in Awala Yalimapo. International teams take part in traditional sports.

Improve your travel photography

Taking pictures is a highlight for many travellers, yet too often the results turn out to be disappointing. Steve Davey, author of Footprint's *Travel Photography*, sets out his top rules for coming home with pictures you can be proud of.

Before you go

Don't waste precious travelling time and do your research before you leave. Find out what festivals or events might be happening or which day the weekly market takes place, and search online image sites such as Flickr to see whether places are best shot at the beginning or end of the day, and what vantage points you should consider.

Get up early

The quality of the light will be better in the few hours after sunrise and again before sunset – especially in the tropics when the sun will be harsh and unforgiving in the middle of the day. Sometimes seeing the sunrise is a part of the whole travel experience: sleep in and you will miss more than just photographs.

Stop and think

Don't just click away without any thought. Pause for a few seconds before raising the camera and ask yourself what you are trying to show with your photograph. Think about what things you need to include in the frame to convey this meaning. Be prepared to move around your subject to get the best angle. Knowing the point of your picture is the first step to making sure that the person looking at the picture will know it too.

Compose your picture

Avoid simply dumping your subject in the centre of the frame every time you take a picture. If you compose with it to one side, then your picture can look more balanced. This will also allow you to show a significant background and make the picture more meaningful. A good rule of thumb is to place your subject or any significant detail a third of the way into the frame; facing into the frame not out of it.

This rule also works for landscapes. Compose with the horizon two-thirds of the way up the frame if the foreground is the most interesting part of the picture; one-third of the way up if the sky is more striking.

Don't get hung up with this so-called Rule of Thirds, though. Exaggerate it by pushing your subject out to the edge of the frame if it makes a more interesting picture; or if the sky is dull in a landscape, try cropping with the horizon near the very top of the frame.

Fill the frame

If you are going to focus on a detail or even a person's face in a close-up portrait, then be bold and make sure that you fill the frame. This is often a case of physically getting in close. You can use a telephoto setting on a zoom lens but this can lead to pictures looking quite flat; moving in close is a lot more fun!

Interact with people

If you want to shoot evocative portraits then it is vital to approach people and seek permission in some way, even if it is just by smiling at someone. Spend a little time with them and they are likely to relax and look less stiff and formal. Action portraits where people are doing something, or environmental portraits, where they are set against a significant background, are a good way to achieve relaxed portraits. Interacting is a good way to find out more about people and their lives, creating memories as well as photographs.

Focus carefully

Your camera can focus quicker than you, but it doesn't know which part of the picture you want to be in focus. If your camera is using the centre focus sensor then move the camera so it is over the subject and half press the button, then, holding it down, recompose the picture. This will lock the focus. Take the now correctly focused picture when you are ready.

Another technique for accurate focusing is to move the active sensor over your subject. Some cameras with touch-sensitive screens allow you to do this by simply clicking on the subject.

Leave light in the sky

Most good night photography is actually taken at dusk when there is some light and colour left in the sky; any lit portions of the picture will balance with the sky and any ambient lighting. There is only a very small window when this will happen, so get into position early, be prepared and keep shooting and reviewing the results. You can take pictures after this time, but avoid shots of tall towers in an inky black sky; crop in close on lit areas to fill the frame.

Bring it home safely

Digital images are inherently ephemeral: they can be deleted or corrupted in a heartbeat. The good news though is they can be copied just as easily. Wherever you travel, you should have a backup strategy. Cloud backups are popular, but make sure that you will have access to fast enough Wi-Fi. If you use RAW format, then you will need some sort of physical back-up. If you don't travel with a laptop or tablet, then you can buy a backup drive that will copy directly from memory cards.

Available in both digital and print formats, Footprint's Travel Photography by Steve Davey covers everything you need to know about travelling with a camera, including simple post-processing. More information is available at www.footprinttravelguides.com

What to do

from remote trekking to cultural tourism

From the tourism point of view, the three Guianas are frequently referred to as the least-explored corner, or best-kept secret of South America. If there is a downside to this it is that services and infrastructure may not match those of some of their larger, more geared-up neighbours. The advantages, though, are many. You are guaranteed adventurous, off-the-beaten-track travel. You will not be sharing the places you visit with crowds of others. Those in the tourism business are truly dedicated and know their country well. Few operators specialize in one type of activity because they sell variations of a number of common themes. In many cases, the lodge that you stay in *is* the destination. Because the lack of development in tourism is matched by a lack of over-exploitation of resources, there are huge areas of wilderness to explore: rainforest, savannah, empty beaches, rapid-strewn rivers. And in those wild places is an equally vast array of wildlife. Not surprisingly, therefore, nature tourism predominates among the main activities in each country.

Many itineraries involve a lot of travelling between places, by rough road, river boat or small plane. Activities can also be fairly demanding in order to make the most of what is to be seen and done (eg early-morning starts, night-time trips, forested mountain hikes). None is excessive, but can be energy-sapping in the heat. While none of the countries has what could be called tropical bathing beaches, there are opportunities for relaxing by a beach on one of the beautiful rivers, taking time out for yoga classes, or learning about traditional crafts and cuisine.

Birdwatching

According to **Avibase**, the World Bird Database (http://avibase.bsc-eoc. org), Guyana has 797 species of bird, Suriname 728 and Guyane 727 (these figures do vary according to source). The three countries combined only have four endemics, indicating that many birds occur in similar habitats elsewhere, but the variety of species is enough to satisfy any birder, whatever his or her experience. Some of the most striking birds are the harpy eagle, Guiana cock-of-the-rock, hoatzin, Guianan red cotinga, crimson fruitcrow, blood-coloured woodpecker, rufous crab-hawk, scarlet ibis and grey-winged trumpeter. Given the number of habitats, though, there are many, many more species worth looking out for, ranging from residents of savannahs, rainforests, mangroves and marshes to migrants, especially on the coast. Hotspots in **Guyana** include Kaieteur National Park, Iwokrama and the Atta lodge and canopy walkway, the Rupununi Savannah, Shell Beach and other parts of the Atlantic coast, even Georgetown itself in the Botanical Gardens. In **Suriname**, hotspots include Brownsberg, renowned for its grey-winged trumpeters, the swamps near the Commewijne plantations, Raleighvallen/Voltzberg in the Central Suriname Nature Reserve and the Sipaliwini savannah in the far south of the reserve. In **Guyane** good birding places include the Ile du Grand Connétable, a seabird reserve to which some tour operators take trips, the Kaw marshes, the Sinnamary estuary and, further west, the Réserve Naturelle Amana, coast paths near Cayenne and the forest near Saül.

Cycling

Suriname is the only country of the three where cycling as a tourist activity is common. Two main companies offer tours and bike hire (**Cardy**, www.cardyadventures.com, and **Fietsen**, www.fietseninsuriname.com), so you can either go on a city tour or a trip to the plantations outside Paramaribo with them (or through another agency), or else rent a bike and pedal off independently. It is possible to cycle from Bonfim, Brazil, to Oiapoque, Brazil, or vice versa, but you need to bear in mind that the paved roads are narrow and in a few places busy; the stretch from Lethem to Linden in Guyana is unpaved, which can be difficult in the wet, and distances between settlements with lodging and food stores are sometimes long; if not camping, couch-surfing or slinging a hammock, accommodation is expensive, as is the cost of meals.

Cultural tourism

Because immigrants of varying nationalities came, or were brought to the Guianas, there are many ethnic groups living alongside the indigenous Amerindian peoples. Consequently, cultural tourism figures prominently in many trips. Lodges in the interior are often adjacent to or run by small communities, either Amerindian or Maroon (escaped slaves), so experiencing that village's customs and traditions is part of the package. The Maroons who welcome tourists are found mostly in Suriname. In the cities one is most aware of the ethnic mix, with African, Asian and, to a lesser extent, European the most visible. The term 'Asian', however, encompasses a variety of people: East Indian, Indo-Pakistani, Javanese in Suriname, Chinese and, in Guyane, Laotian. The main religions are Christian, Hindu and Muslim and often different places of worship are in close proximity.

A further aspect is the great variety of foods that you will find, reflecting both the culinary traditions of the Amerindian people and the origins of the immigrants: Indian, Africa, Créole, Chinese, English, Portuguese, French cuisine in Guyane, and North American.

And don't forget rum. The Guianas produce some of the finest rum in the world and distilleries run tours. For more details see Food and drink, page 21.

Fishing

Sport fishing is available in all three countries – not surprising in countries with so many rivers teeming with fish. Also Suriname has the Brokopondo reservoir, where fishing is a popular activity. Peacock bass and various types of catfish are sought-after catches. **Rewa Eco-Lodge** (Guyana) specializes in conservation of the arapaima, one of the largest freshwater fish in the world. They run catch-and-release fishing expeditions at certain times of year.

Trekking

Trekking is almost exclusively on an organized basis since a guide is essential in the rainforest. Many treks are of a few hours, such as those from lodges in the Rupununi and from Iwokrama (Guyana) and around Brownsberg and up the Voltzberg mountain (Suriname). The most celebrated multi-day trip is the overland route to the Kaieteur Falls in Guyana (see page 33).

Wildlife

Viewing birds (see above) is not the only wildlife experience in the Guianas. Mammals, reptiles, plants and insects (not just the ones that bite) are relatively easy to spot, especially when expert guides can lead you to the places where such creatures are found. There is a much-vaunted list of the 'giants of the Guianas', a couple of which have already been mentioned above (harpy eagle, arapaima). Others are jaguar, giant river otter, giant anteater, giant river turtle, black caiman, anaconda and giant Victoria amazonica waterlily. Other superlatives include the greenheart tree with its incredibly hard and durable wood, the false vampire bat (the largest in the Americas), the capybara (the largest rodent), the bird-eating spider and the bullet ant, said to have the most painful sting of any. Add in frequent sightings of monkeys (or hearings in the case of howlers), elusive cats, sloths, marine turtles, colourful amphibians such as the tiny golden frog that lives only in the tank bromeliads at Kaieteur, countless butterflies and the plantlife of the rainforest, savannah and coast and you have an unmatched wildlife destination, whichever of the three countries you decide to visit.

Where to stay

from gîtes and lodges to hostels and hammocks

Guyana

Georgetown has the widest range of accommodation options in the country, catering for local and international business travellers as well as tourists. A few are affiliated with global brands, but most are Guyanese establishments. There are many mid-price hotels (our $$$-$$ range, see box, below), but fewer at the cheaper end. It is advisable to make a reservation in advance. Almost all hotels in Georgetown have electricity generators, water pumps and overhead tanks to deal with any interruptions in supply. When booking an air-conditioned room, ensure it also has natural ventilation. Towns outside the capital have reasonable places to stay, but less choice.

Many hotels are members of the **Tourism and Hospitality Association of Guyana** (**THAG**) ⓘ *Private Sector Commission Building, Waterloo St, North Cummingsburg, Georgetown, T225 0807, www.exploreguyana.org.*

In the interior, accommodation is in lodges. These rarely have many rooms, catering for small groups only. Because there is no alternative, they are exclusive, but that does not make them super-luxurious or unwelcoming. Rooms are generally comfortable, with a shower attached. They may be quite rustic, with thatched roofs, and it is likely that you will share with some forms of wildlife (insects and bats, mostly). Beds have mosquito nets and many places provide insect repellent (although you should still bring your own),

---

Price codes

Where to stay	Restaurants
$$$$ over US$150	$$$ over US$12
$$$ US$66-150	$$ US$7-12
$$ US$30-65	$ US$6 and under
$ under US$30	
Price of a double room in high season, including taxes.	Price for a two-course meal for one person, excluding drinks or service charge.

drinking water and emergency whistles. Meals are served communally and the kitchen team will explain to you the food that you have been served. Lodges are invariably owned and operated by, or are closely associated with a community (Amerindian in Guyana, Maroon or Amerindian in Suriname). This means that many of the activities at the lodge are tied to the community, that guides are local and that the village's culture is shared and preserved. One model for community-based tourism is that everything is shared by the community. Projects in the village, including health, benefit from the profits generated by the lodge. Tourism is run by a committee which reports to the community council and village captain (*toshao* in Guyana). The lodge is run by a team of staff who work for a month, to be replaced by another team the following month, and so on.

Suriname

Paramaribo, like Georgetown, has the greatest choice, from a couple of backpacker-style hostels to top-of-the-range hotels and resorts. Most, even the hostels, are in our $$$-$$ range. Hotels (and restaurants) are rare outside Paramaribo, but accommodation in the interior is excellent if organized through a tour operator. (See above for lodge accommodation.) Many operators have their own resorts. In some cases, for instance national park lodges run by Stinasu (see page 73), you can choose to go independently rather than all-inclusive. You still have to reserve accommodation, maybe supply your own hammock and mosquito net, but you must take all your food and drink and arrange transport. A tent is less useful in this climate. Do not travel independently without taking some local currency.

In 2016 the **Suriname Hospitality and Tourism Association** ⓘ *SHATA, Kristalstraat 1, Paramaribo, T710 0823, www.shata.sr,* was formed, initially with 22 members.

Guyane

There are few hotels under our $$$ bracket and almost no restaurants below the $$$ bracket. Accommodation in Guyane is more expensive than Paris, but food is better value. The **Comité du Tourisme de la Guyane** ⓘ *12 rue Lallouette, BP 801, 97300 Cayenne, T296500, www.guyane-amazonie.fr,* has addresses of furnished apartments for rent (*locations clévacances*) and gîtes, with accommodation in hammocks or *carbets* (imitation Amerindian huts), *carbets d'hôtes,* which include breakfast, and *camps touristiques.*

Food
& drink

a cosmopolitan cuisine ... and rum

Guyana

The blend of different cultural influences (see Cultural tourism, page 17) gives distinctive flavour to Guyanese cuisine. One well-known dish, traditional at Christmas but available at other times, is pepper-pot (see Menu reader, page 22).

Some popular local dishes are cook-up-rice, *dhal pouri* or *roti* and *metagee*. All are available in Créole restaurants. Seafood is plentiful and varied, as are tropical fruits and vegetables. The staple food is rice. In the interior wild meat is often available, eg wild cow, or *labba* (a small rodent).

Rum is the most popular drink. There is a wide variety of brands, all cheap, including the best which are very good and cost US$3.50 a bottle. **Demerara Distillers Ltd** produces several prize-winning brands, from three- to 21-year-old rums. Their 15-year-old *El Dorado* has frequently been voted the best rum in the world. **Demerara Distillers** have a distillery tour and visit to their rum heritage, US$15. High wine is a strong local rum. There is also local brandy and whisky (Diamond Club), which are worth trying. *D'Aguiar's Cream Liqueur*, produced and bottled by **Banks DIH Ltd**, is excellent (and strong). The local beer, **Banks**, made partly from rice, is good and cheap. There is a wide variety of fruit juices produced by **Topco**. *Mauby*, a local drink brewed from the bark of a tree, and natural cane juice are delightful thirst quenchers available from Créole restaurants and local vendors.

Suriname

Surinamese cuisine is as rich and varied as the country's ethnic makeup. High-quality rice is the main staple. Cassava, sweet potatoes, plantain and hot red peppers are widely used. See Menu reader, page 22. Among Suriname's many tropical fruits, palm nuts such as the orange-coloured *awarra* and the cone-shaped brown *maripa* are most popular.

The local beer is called Parbo and the best-selling rums are Borgoe, Mariënburg and Black Cat, all distilled by **Suriname Alcoholic Beverages**

Menu reader

Guyana

cook-up-rice one-pot Guyanese rice dish that is generally made at the weekend.

mauby a local drink brewed from the bark of a tree.

metagee a stew of meat, fish and dumplings with coconut and vegetables.

pepper-pot meat cooked in bitter cassava juice (*casareep*) with peppers and herbs.

Suriname

awarra orange coloured palm nuts.

bami Indonesian fried noodles (spicy and slightly sweet).

moksie alesie rice mixed with meat, smoked chicken and fish, white beans, tomatoes, peppers and spices.

nasi goreng Indonesian fried rice (spicy and slightly sweet).

okersoep met tayerblad gumbo and cassava soup.

petjil cooked vegetables served with peanut sauce.

phulawri Hindustani fried chickpea balls.

pindasoep peanut soup with plantain dumplings or noodles.

pom a puree of the *tayer* root (a relative of cassava) tastily spiced and served with chicken.

Guyane

blaff a spicy fish soup, usually served at the start of the day.

boucanage meat or fish steamed in banana leaves.

bouillon d'aoura a slow-cooked stew containing crab meat and other seafood, chicken, vegetables and palm fruit.

couac grated, dried yucca served as an accompaniment.

fricasée rice, beans and meat (often wild game).

(SAB) ⓘ *www.sabrum.com*. There are many fruit juices to sample, as well as the various non-alcoholic drinks of the different ethnic communities.

Guyane

As in Guyana and Suriname, different cultures have given an individual character to the cuisine, although the French influence is ever-present. The main ingredients are seafood, shrimp, rice, vegetables and spices (one of the many hot peppers available is named after the capital, Cayenne, after all). Many restaurants in Cayenne serve a varied menu of seafood, meat and chicken dishes, but also pizza, pasta, burgers, etc. Other influences are Chinese (often the cheapest), Vietnamese, Indonesian, Indian, Créole and Spanish. Some dishes to look out for are *bouillon d'aoura*, *blaff*, *fricassée*, *couac* and *boucanage*.

The most popular drink is Ti' Punch, a cocktail of rum, lime and sugar syrup. Cayenne has several French-style patisseries and cafés. Rhum Saint-Maurice, from near St-Laurent du Maroni, is the local rum distillery. The local artisanal beer is brewed by Jeune Gueule (1749 Chemin de l'Egyptienne, Matoury, T380174, www.jeunegueule.com): Blaka, 8°; Orpailleuse, 6°; Weïty, 5°; and Blonde, 4.5°, in 33 cl bottles.

Guyana

Highlights of Guyana include the Kaieteur Falls, among the highest in the world, the Orinduik Falls on the border with Brazil and the Iwokrama Rainforest Reserve, with the Iwokrama Canopy Walkway. Travelling on any of the rivers, many with excellent beaches, is the most interesting way to get around. On the coast there are few beaches for bathing, but in the far northwest is Shell Beach, a protected area for marine turtles and birdlife.

Georgetown

tree-lined streets and traditional wooden great houses

Guyana's capital (population 200,000) and chief town and port is on the east bank of the mouth of the Demerara river. The climate is tropical, with a mean temperature of 27°C, but the trade winds provide welcome relief. The city is built on a grid plan, with wide tree-lined streets and drainage canals following the layout of the old sugar estates. Parts of the city are very attractive, with a profusion of flowering trees and white-painted wooden 19th-century houses raised on stilts. In the evening the sea wall is crowded with strollers, and at Easter it is a mass of colourful kites.

St George's Anglican Cathedral and around

Although part of the old centre was destroyed by fire in 1945, there are some fine 19th-century buildings, particularly on or near High Street and the Avenue of the Republic. St George's Anglican Cathedral, which dates from 1889, is 44 m high and is said to be the world's tallest free-standing wooden building. It was designed by Sir Arthur Blomfield, who placed the supporting columns either side of the altar, leaving nothing but open space between ceiling and floor. Above the altar is a chandelier given by Queen Victoria. Other fine buildings on High Street are the Gothic-style **City Hall** (1888), the **City Engineer's Office**, the **Victoria Law Courts** (1887) and the **Magistrates' Court**. The **Public Buildings**, on Brickdam, which house Parliament, are an impressive neoclassical structure built in 1839. Opposite is **St Andrew's Presbytery** (18th century). **State House** on Main Street is the residence of the president. Much of the city centre is dominated by the imposing tower above **Stabroek market** (1881). At the head of Brickdam is an aluminium arch commemorating independence. Nearby is a monument to the 1763 slave

Essential Guyana

Finding your feet

Cheddi Jagan International Airport is at Timehri, 40 km south of Georgetown, while **Ogle International Airport** is 8 km from the city. Taxis and minibuses run to Georgetown from both.

Fact file
Location 5.0000° N, 58.7500° W
Capital Georgetown
Time zone GMT -4 hrs
Telephone country code +592
Currency Guyanese dollars (GYD)

Getting around

There are domestic flights, some scheduled, some charters, to several parts of the country. The main roads from Georgetown to Linden and to Springlands for the ferry to Suriname are paved. The unpaved road that continues from Linden to Lethem gives access to places along the way to Brazil, but many other places are only reachable by boat.

Tip...
There are ATMs in Georgetown, but as a back up you are advised to take cash dollars or euros.

Safety

Georgetown is a beautiful city, but check with your hotel, tour operator, the police or government authorities about unsafe areas. Don't walk the streets at night: always take a taxi, especially if going to Sheriff Street for the nightlife. At all times, avoid Albouystown (south of the centre) and the Tiger Bay area, just one block west of Main Street. Leave your valuables in your hotel. These problems are restricted to Georgetown and nearby villages; the interior remains as safe as ever.

Weather Guyana

	January	February	March	April	May	June
High	30°C	30°C	31°C	31°C	31°C	31°C
Low	22°C	22°C	22°C	23°C	23°C	23°C
Rain	263mm	96mm	86mm	178mm	310mm	305mm

	July	August	September	October	November	December
High	31°C	32°C	33°C	33°C	32°C	30°C
Low	23°C	23°C	23°C	23°C	23°C	23°C
Rain	262mm	139mm	96mm	114mm	151mm	238mm

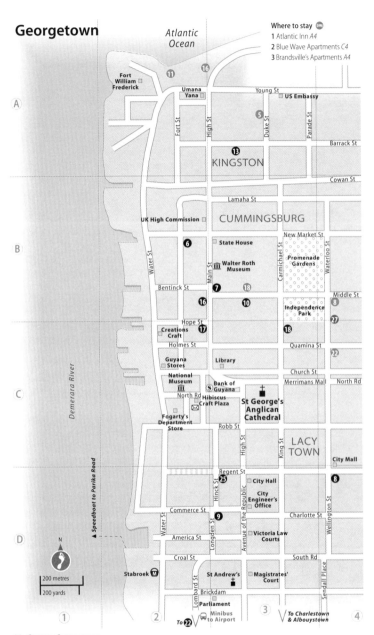

Georgetown

Atlantic Ocean

Fort William Frederick

Umana Yana

Young St

US Embassy

Fort St
High St
Duke St
Parade St

Barrack St

5

13 KINGSTON

Cowan St

Lamaha St

UK High Commission

CUMMINGSBURG

New Market St

Carmichael St
Waterloo St

Promenade Gardens

6 State House

Main St

🏛 Walter Roth Museum

Bentinck St

7 **18**

Middle St

8

16 **10**

Independence Park

Water St

Hope St

Creations Craft

17

18

27

Holmes St

Guyana Stores

Library

Quamina St

22

Church St

National Museum 🏛

Merrimans Mall

North Rd

Bank of Guyana 💲

Hibiscus Craft Plaza

St George's Anglican Cathedral

Fogarty's Department Store

High St
King St

Robb St

LACY TOWN

City Mall

Regent St

25

City Hall

8

Hinck St

Avenue of the Republic

City Engineer's Office

Commerce St

9

Charlotte St

Wellington St

Water St

Longden St

America St

Victoria Law Courts

Croal St

South Rd

Sendall Place

N ↑

200 metres
200 yards

▲ Speedboat to Parika Road

Stabroek Ⓜ

St Andrew's ✝

Magistrates' Court

Lombard St

Brickdam

Parliament

🚌 Minibus to Airport

To **22**

V To Charlestown & Albouystown

Demerara River

1

2

3

4

rebellion, surmounted by an impressive statue of Cuffy, its best-known leader. Near the **Pegasus** hotel on Seawall Road is the **Umana Yana**, a conical thatched structure built by a group of Wai Wai Amerindians using traditional techniques for the 1972 conference of the Non-Aligned Movement (it burnt down in 2014 and was rebuilt in 2016). The **National Museum** ⓘ *North Rd, opposite the post office, T225 7191, Mon-Fri 0900-1600, Sat 0900-1400, free,* has exhibits from Guyana and elsewhere, including a model of Georgetown before the fire and a good natural history section. The **Walter Roth Museum of Anthropology** ⓘ *61 Main St, T225 8486, Mon-Thu 0800-1630, Fri 0800-1530,* has artefacts from Guyana's nine Amerindian tribes and serves as a research centre for indigenous people.

Botanical Gardens and around

The **Botanical Gardens** ⓘ *20 mins' walk east from the Anglican Cathedral, free,* covering 50 ha, have Victorian bridges and pavilions, palms and lily ponds (undergoing continual improvements). The gardens are safe in daylight hours, but keep to the marked paths. Do not go there after dark. Near the southwest corner is the former residence of the president, **Castellani House** ⓘ *Vlissengen Rd and Homestretch Av, T225 0579, Mon-Fri 1000-1700, Sat 1400-1800,* which now houses the renovated **National Art Collection**, and there is also a large **mausoleum** containing the remains of the former president, Forbes Burnham, which is decorated with reliefs depicting scenes from his political career. Look out for the rare cannonball tree (*Couroupita guianensis*), named after the appearance of its poisonous fruit. The Botanical Gardens offer great birdwatching. The city has 200 bird species from 39 families, many of which can be seen in the gardens. Flycatchers, tanagers, hummingbirds and many migrating species such as peregrine falcons and warblers can be found around the capital, but the true stars are the blood-coloured woodpecker, which is endemic to the Guiana Shield, and the festive parrot. Both are regularly spotted in the gardens. Tour operators offer birdwatching tours.

The **zoo** ⓘ *Vlissengen Rd and Regent Rd, T225 9142, 0930-1730, US$1.50 for adults, half price for children; US$11 to use personal video*, is being upgraded, together with the Botanical Gardens and National Park. It carries the WWF logo and has educational programmes. It has a collection of local animals including manatees, which can be seen throughout the day. The zoo also boasts a breeding centre for endangered birds which are released into the wild. Nearby is the **National Cultural Centre**, an impressive air-conditioned theatre with a large stage. Performances are also given at the **Theatre Guild Playhouse** in Parade Street. There are also beautiful tropical plants in the **Promenade Gardens** ⓘ *Middle St, open 0830-1630.* Also in the centre are the **Indian Monument Gardens** ⓘ *Camp and Church St*, with the **Indian Heritage Monument** representing the *Whitby*, one of the ships that transported indentured labourers from India to Guyana in 1838. **Indian Arrival Day** is celebrated here on 5 May and it is the site for other Hindu festivals such as **Phagwah** and **Divali**. More tropical gardens are in the **National Park** on Carifesta Avenue, which has a good public running track. At the Kitty Seawall, Carifesta Avenue, is the **1823 Slave Rebellion Monument** commemorating the 1823 Demerara slave uprising, with a sculpture by Ivor Thom of an African slave holding a cutlass, chain and cross to represent rebellion, revolution and religion.

Georgetown Cricket Club

The Georgetown Cricket Club at Bourda is one of the finest cricket grounds in the tropics and is perhaps the oldest ground in the Caribbean, formally opened in 1885. Near the Botanical Gardens, between North Road and Regent Road, it is moated to prevent flooding as it is below sea level. For the ICC World Cup in 2007, a new stadium was built at Providence on the east bank of Demerara right next to **Ramada Georgetown Princess Hotel** (8 km from the city on the airport road; take bus 42 or a taxi). It has fine modern stands but not enough protection from sun and rain. Regional cricket is still played at Bourda, but its future is uncertain.

Outside Georgetown

overwhelming landscapes, wildlife, village life and working ranches

The interior of Guyana is a land of great rivers, dramatic waterfalls, rainforests and savannahs. On the coast are turtle-nesting grounds and sea defences. You can stay at working ranches and community-run lodges. At all times, expect superb nature watching, good guiding and welcoming service.

Southeast to Suriname

New Amsterdam and the Berbice river ⓘ *From Georgetown, take a minibus (No 50) or collective taxi to Rosignol on the west bank of the Berbice, US$6, then cross the river.* A floating bridge goes from Cotton Tree to Palmyra Village (5 km from New Amsterdam); a toll is charged. On the east bank of the Berbice river, near its mouth and at the junction with the Canje river, is picturesque New Amsterdam, just over 100 km southeast of the capital. Originally built by the Dutch, Nieuw Amsterdam was made the seat of Dutch colonial rule in 1790, but it lost its status in the early 19th century when the British had taken over the colony. A few Dutch buildings remain but much of the fine architecture is from the 19th century.

Corriverton The road continues east from New Amsterdam (minibus No 50, US$3) to Springlands and Skeldon at the mouth of the Corentyne river. The towns are officially known as Corriverton (Corentyne River Town). Springlands is 2 km long, so you need to know where you want to get off the bus. You'll find the **Republic Bank** and **Guyana National Commercial Bank**, and Suriname dollars can officially be changed into Guyanese dollars here.

Near Corriverton is No **63 Beach** (**Berbice**), part of a 16-km stretch of coast that includes 12 villages. Thousands of visitors come here each weekend to swim and play volleyball, softball cricket and other sports. There are changing facilities, *benabs* (shelters) and washrooms.

Border with Suriname A ferry sails once or twice daily from Moleson, or Crabwood Creek, 13 km south of Springlands, to South Drain/Canawaima in Suriname, 40 km south of Nieuw-Nickerie (see Transport, below). **Suriname Embassy** ⓘ *in Georgetown: 54 New Garden and Anira St, Queenstown, T226 7844, or 225 2631, surnmemb@gol.net.gy.* The consular section is open Monday, Wednesday, Friday morning only, but visa applications can be handed in at any time. In 2017 finance was being sought for a bridge across the Corentyne.

West from Georgetown

The road crosses the 2-km-long floating **Demerara bridge** made of steel pontoons (opens often for shipping, schedules given on www.harbourbridge.gov.gy; US$0.50-1 for private vehicles, pedestrians free). Speedboats cross the Demerara from Stabroek market (US$0.50 every 30 minutes).

The road continues 42 km, past rice paddies, kokers and through villages to **Parika**, a growing town on the east bank of the Essequibo river (minibus US$2.50). It has a Sunday market, 0600-1100, and three banks. Two ferries, the *Kanawan* and *Sabanto*, cross the river to **Supenaam** on the west bank at high tide, mostly twice a day, US$1.50 (schedules can be checked at the **Transport and Harbours Department**, T225 9355, or T225 9350); or speedboat US$5 (can be very wet).

On **Tiger Island** at the mouth of the Essequibo is popular **Hamburg Beach**. On the first Monday in August some 15,000 people arrive for the **Hamburg Beach Fête**, to celebrate **Emancipation Day**.

From Supenaam, minibuses or taxis (US$7.50 per person) go to **Charity through Adventure** and **Anna Regina**. Nearby there is a resort at **Lake Mainstay**, see below. You can visit a hot and cold lake, which varies in temperature according to depth, and the **Whyaka Amerindian Community**, 13 km from Anna Regina.

Mainstay is 2¾ hours by road and ferry from Georgetown (depending on tides). The road goes on to **Charity**, a pleasant town with loud bars, various hotels and a lively market on Monday (quiet at other times).

Border with Venezuela Near the border with Venezuela are the small ports of **Morawhanna** (Morajuana to the Venezuelans) and **Mabaruma**. Mabaruma has replaced Morawhanna as capital of the region since it is at less at risk from flooding. If arriving from Venezuela, make sure that the official who stamps your passport is not an imposter. You may only be given a five-day temporary visa, to be renewed on arrival in Georgetown. **Venezuelan Embassy** ⓘ *in Georgetown: 296 Thomas St, South Cummingsburg, T226 6749, http://guyana.embajada.gob.ve, Mon-Fri 0830-1630*. It is not normally possible to cross from Guyana to Venezuela.

Shell Beach Part of a protected area of Atlantic coastline, Shell Beach is some 145 km long, from the Pomeroon river to the Venezuelan border. It safeguards the nesting grounds of leatherback, green, hawksbill and olive ridley turtles. Nesting activity begins in late March and continues, with hatching, until mid-August. Former

> **Note...**
> At the time of writing there were no tours to Shell Beach as the area was experiencing problems with flooding and erosion.

turtle hunters have been retrained to patrol and identify nest sites, which are logged using global positioning satellite equipment. The project receives support from the WWF. The coast consists of areas of mangrove swamps with beaches formed entirely of eroded shell particles. There are large flocks of scarlet ibis. Other birds include Amazon parrots, macaws, toucans, woodpeckers and crab hawks. Iguanas are usually seen in the mangroves, with sightings of rare river dolphin on the narrower stretches of river.

The camp consists of a thatched dining area and huts for the staff and igloo-type tents for guests, with fly-sheets and mosquito netting (vital in the rainy season, when there are 'blizzards' of mosquitoes). Showers and toilets are basic. Food is very good. An Arawak family runs the camp and offers daily activities of fishing and birdwatching. They are excellent English-speaking guides. Turtle watching is available in season.

Fort Island and Bartica From Parika (see page 31) a vehicle ferry runs up the Essequibo river to Bartica daily at 0400 (returns 1200), US$2.50 one way. The 58-km journey takes six hours, stopping at **Fort Island**; boats come out from riverside settlements to load up with fruit. River taxis run from Parika to Bartica all day, US$12.50 per person. There are also flights from Ogle five days a week (see Transport, page 52). On Fort Island is a **Dutch fort** (built 1743, restored by Raleigh

International in 1991) and the **Dutch Court of Policy**, built at the same time. There is also a small village; the rest of the island is dairy farms.

Bartica, at the junction of the Essequibo and Mazaruni rivers, is the 'take-off' town for the gold and diamond fields and the interior generally. Opposite Bartica, at the mouth of the Mazaruni, is **Kaow Island**, with a lumber mill. The *stelling* (wharf) and **market** in Bartica are very colourful. Bars flank the main street. The annual Easter **regatta** is a boisterous affair featuring watersports, mostly power-boat racing, other sports, a parade and a beauty pageant. There are several resorts nearby; see Where to stay, page 40.

Southwest of Bartica The Essequibo is navigable to large boats for some miles upstream of Bartica. The Cuyuni flows into the Mazaruni three miles above Bartica, and above this confluence the Mazaruni is impeded for 190 km by thousands of islands, rapids and waterfalls. To avoid this stretch of treacherous river a poor road runs from Bartica to Issano, where boats can be taken up the more tranquil upper Mazaruni. At the confluence of the Mazaruni and Cuyuni rivers are the remains of the early 17th-century Dutch stronghold **Kyk-over-al**, once the seat of government for the Dutch county of Essequibo. Nearby are the **Marshall Falls** (30-60 minutes by boat from Bartica, included in Essequibo river day trips, otherwise you have to hire a boat, US$250 per boat for a group of six to eight, return), which are beautiful, but too dangerous for swimming. You can swim in the nearby bay, part of the **Rainbow River Marshall Falls** property (day trippers may have to pay an entrance fee).

Kaieteur National Park ① *Permission to enter the park must be obtained from the National Parks Commission, Georgetown, T225 9142, entry costs US$15 (both arranged by tour operators); a guide costs US$22.50.* The **Kaieteur Falls**, on the Potaro river, nearly five times the height of Niagara, with a drop of 228 m, are almost 100 m wide. Ranking with the Victoria and Iguazú Falls in majesty and beauty, they have the added attraction of being surrounded by unspoilt forest. Lying within a national park, there is also plenty of wildlife: tapirs, ocelots, monkeys, armadillos, anteaters and birds. At the falls themselves, one can see the magnificent silver fox, the Guianan cock-of-the-rock and the white-collared swift, also known as Makonaima bird, which lives behind the falls. At dusk the swifts swoop in and out of the gorge before passing through the deluge to roost behind the water. February is the best month for seeing the cock-of-the-rock dancing to attract the grey-green female. The golden rocket frog lives in the giant tank bromeliad and is endemic to this area. The tank bromeliads flower May-June and the microhabitat within the leaf structure is rich in species. Tours of the park must be accompanied by a guide, either from an accredited tour operator or a ranger from the park's Kaieteur office, but they usually have one of each. There are four viewpoints, but that closest to the falls, beside the lip, was temporarily closed in 2016-2017 (it is not known when it will reopen). Visitors normally start at **Johnson's View**, the furthest from the falls, then go to **Boy Scouts' View**, then **Rainbow View**, from where you can often see rainbows in the spray. In the dry

months, April and October, the flow of the falls is reduced; in January and June/July the flow is fullest. In the height of the wet season (June), the overland route is difficult and not recommended.

The overland route from Georgetown to Kaieteur takes three to five days. Some parts of the trip are challenging. The first part is by road to **Pamela Landing**, via Linden, the Essequibo ferry and Mahdia. From Pamela Landing a boat goes to the first night's lodging in hammocks near the **Amatuk Falls**. Next day is either by boat or on foot to a hammock site at **Waratuk Falls**. From there it's a walk and boat ride to **Tukeit**, where there is a guesthouse/hammock site. Some tours continue the same day up the **Oh My God** ascent to the top of Kaieteur Falls, three to four hours, others relax at Tukeit before the climb.

The **Pakaraima Mountains** stretch from Kaieteur westwards to include the highest peak in Guyana, **Mount Roraima**, once believed to be the inspiration for Conan Doyle's *Lost World*. Roraima is very difficult to climb from the Guyanese side, but **Wilderness Explorers** offer trips via Brazil and Venezuela.

Orinduik Falls Orinduik Falls are on the Ireng river, which forms the border with Brazil; the river pours over steps and terraces of jasper, with a backdrop of the Pakaraima Mountains. There is good swimming at the falls which are a 25-minute flight from Kaieteur.

South from Georgetown: to Brazil
Linden The second-largest town in Guyana is a bauxite mining town on the banks of the Demerara river. The road from the capital is good (slow for the first part to Timehri); police checks are to stop drug and gun running. Linden's opencast mine is 60-90 m deep and is said to have the world's longest boom walking dragline. The town is dominated by a disused alumina plant and scarred by old bauxite pits. In town is the lovely colonial guesthouse on the Demerara river, run by the mining company.

From Linden, rough roads suitable for 4WD vehicles run south to the bauxite mining towns of Ituni and Kwakwani. A good road goes west from Linden to Rockstone ferry on Essequibo river. From Rockstone roads run north to Bartica and southwest to Issano. The main road south to the logging centre at Mabura Hill is in excellent condition; from here a good road runs west to Mahdia, with a pontoon crossing of the Essequibo, and another road continues south from Mabura Hill to Kurupukari, the Essequibo river crossing on the route to Lethem. Over the river you enter Iwokrama.

Iwokrama ⓘ *For information and prices, which change frequently, contact the administrator, Iwokrama International Centre for Rainforest Conservation and Development, 77 High St, Kingston, Georgetown, T225 1504, http://iwokrama.org. Rates for lodging and tour packages are given on http://iwokramariverlodge.com. The northern entrance is open 0600-1800; the southern entrance 0430-1630, see Transport, page 55.* This is a 371,345-ha project set up by Guyana and the Commonwealth to conserve tropical forest primarily, but other habitats as well.

The name means 'place of refuge'. As well as conservation, the programme involves studies on the sustainable use of the rainforest and ecotourism. It is hoped that the results will provide a database for application worldwide. The **Field Station** is at **Kurukupari**, near the Arawak village of **Fairview** (which has an airstrip), on the northeastern boundary of the reserve. You can meet research teams, take boat trips and stay at satellite camps deep in the forest (**Clearwater** on the Burro-burro, **Kabocalli** and **Turtle Mountain** on the Essequibo). Well-trained rangers, who speak their native language and English, escort visitors through the forest on many trails. One goes to **Turtle Mountain** (45 minutes by boat, then 1½ hours' walk), go early for great views of the forest canopy. Another trek is to the top of **Mount Iwokrama**, a difficult 20-km round trip; for the less fit there is a 10-km trail to the foot of the mountain to a pleasant stream and Amerindian petroglyphs. Jaguars and other cats may be seen, there are four species of monkey, bats are an important subject of study and there is excellent birdwatching. One trail, whose entrance is only known by guides, leads to a cock-of-the-rock nest which has been in use for at least 10 years. The nearby lek is the site of the male bird's dancing in February. Fishing is good, especially for peacock bass. There are set rates for boat and Land Rover use and for field assistants to accompany you.

Note...
For visiting many parts of the interior, particularly Amerindian districts, permits are required in advance from the village council. If on a tour, the operator will take care of this. If travelling independently you can book with one of the many lodges as most work directly with the village councils. To conduct scientific, anthropological or archaeological research, permission is needed from the village council and the Ministry of Indigenous People's Affairs (251-252 Quamina St, South Cummingsburg, Georgetown, T227 5067, http://indigenous peoples.gov.gy). If in doubt, check beforehand with the ministry.

There is a 33-m-high **Iwokrama Canopy Walkway** ⓘ *US$25 pp (children under 13, US$18) for a day visit including entry to the walkway and qualified guide with good birding knowledge, www.iwokramacanopywalkway.com*, managed by **Wilderness Explorers**, **Surama**, **Rock View Lodge** and **Iwokrama International Centre**, under the name of **Community And Tourism Services (CATS)**; but any tour operator can make bookings. The walkway allows visitors to walk among the treetops and see the birds and monkeys of the upper canopy. Night excursions are available on the walkway. There is a library with birding books and a small arts and crafts shop. See **Atta Rainforest Lodge**, page 43, which gives good access to wildlife in addition to the canopy walkway, with lots of guides.

Just beyond the southern entrance to Iwokrama a road turns west to the Makushi Amerindian village of **Surama** which organizes its own ecotourism activities through the village council and can accommodate guests in the **Eco-Lodge** ⓘ *http://suramaecolodge.com, bookings through the website or through the CATS partnership (see above)*. It is in a lovely location some distance from the village, overlooking both savannah and forest. The lodge is more

rustic than some others, but is still comfortable with en suite benabs and, in the main building, good food in the restaurant and a handicrafts and hammock area upstairs. The office, 150 m away, has Wi-Fi. Overnight accommodation is $ per person and there are tours ranging from two days/one night to six days/five nights (US$209-660, all options listed on website). Birdwatching, night trekking and boating are arranged and guides are included in the price. The staff are very helpful and knowledgeable. A harpy eagle nest nearby has proven very reliable over the last five years, with good sightings. The forest is beautiful, with many animals especially at dawn on the dirt road between Surama and the Lethem–Georgetown road, but one of the main attractions is that the Eco-Lodge allows you to experience both forest and savannah in one place.

Rupununi Savannah This is an extensive area of dry grassland in the far southwest of Guyana, with scattered trees, termite mounds and wooded hills. The rivers, creeks and ponds, lined with Ite palms and other trees, are good for seeing wildlife. Among a wide variety of birds, look out for macaws,

> **Fact...**
> 'Ponds' have water permanently, while ponds that dry out are called 'bashes'.

toucan, parrots, parakeets, osprey, hawks and jabiru storks (take binoculars). Many of the animals are nocturnal and seldom seen. The region is scattered with Amerindian villages and a few large cattle ranches which date from the late 19th century: the descendants of some of the Scottish settlers still live here. Links with Brazil are much closer than they are with the Guyanese coast; many people speak Portuguese and most trade is with Brazil. See http://rupununi.org.

In the wet season (May to July/August), much of the savannah may flood and malaria mosquitoes and kabura/sandflies are widespread, but there is also a profusion of beautiful wildflowers. The best time to visit is October to April. Some years there is Christmas rain. River bathing is good, but beware of dangerous stingrays and black caiman. Note that in many villages you will have to get permission from the village council or the captain, *toshao*, to visit and you may have to pay a small fee, unless on tours organized by operators or lodges, when permission will already have been obtained in advance.

Several lodges in the Rupununi are on or near the Rupununi river and travelling by boat is a lovely way to get between them. Organized tours invariably include more than one lodge and transport will involve road and boat, or plane and boat, sometimes all three. See Where to stay, page 43.

Annai Some 25 km south of Surama, this Amerindian village is located in the northern savannahs, south of the Iwokrama Rainforest Programme. Annai's airstrip is close to **Rock View Lodge**, which is most convenient for visiting the North Rupununi owing to its proximity to the Georgetown–Lethem road and the Rupununi river (see Where to stay and Transport, pages 44 and 55). It is possible to trek from Annai over the plains to the Rupununi river, or through dense jungle to the mountains. By the turn-off to Annai is Aranaputa, a village with

community-run tourism projects such as the Clarence Mountain Nature Trail and riding on the savannah, but visitors may recognize it best from the peanut butter served widely in the region and made in the village by a women's cooperative. **Kwatamang Landing**, east of Annai, is a suitable access point to the Rupununi river for all the lodges from Iwokrama to Rewa, Karanambu and Caiman House at Yupukari. Between Wowetta on the main road and Kwatamang is Bina Hill, where a community initiative set up a tertiary level education system with courses on agriculture, tourism, carpentry, English, maths and more, with its own Paiwomak radio station and dormitories for students.

Lethem A small but scattered town on the Brazilian border (see below), this is the service centre for the Rupununi and a shopping centre with supermarkets, shoe and clothing stores for the people of the savannah and for Brazilians. There are ATMs, a small **hospital** ① T772 2006, a **police station** ① T772 2011, and government offices. The road into town divides, one branch heading towards the international bridge, the other turning left onto the street lined with most of the stores, which skirts the airport on one side and the main part of town on the other. The road ends at the roundabout by **Takutu** hotel and petrol station. A left turn here leads to the entrance to the airport. Prices are about twice as high as in Georgetown.

> **Fact...**
> In Lethem, a big event at Easter is the rodeo, from the Tuesday of Holy Week until the Wednesday after, visited by cowboys from all over the Rupununi.

About 2.5 km south of town in the village of **St Ignatius** there is a Jesuit mission dating from 1911. From Lethem, transport can be hired for day-trips to the **Moco-Moco Falls** and the **Kumu Falls** (4WD and driver to Moco-Moco US$60-70, long, rough ride and walk, but worth it). The nearby **Kanuku mountains**, about two hours away (transport can be hired to here also), are recognized by **Conservation International** as one of the few remaining pristine Amazonian areas. There is good bird and mammal watching, adventure tourism and there are waterfalls to visit. The mountains were made a protected area in 2016 under the auspices of the national and regional governments, Conservation International and the 18 Makushi and Wapishana communities of the **Kanuku Mountain Community Representative Group**. Kanuku is said to be the most ecologyically diverse region in Guyana with 70% of all mammals and 53% of all birds that live in the country.

Border with Brazil The **Takutu river** separates Lethem from Bonfim in Brazil. The crossing is about 1.6 km north of Lethem and 2.5 km from Bonfim. The river is crossed by a bridge, before which one lane of the road crosses over the other so that traffic is on the correct side of the road for the neighbouring country (left in Guyana, right in Brazil). Formalities are tight on both sides of the border and it is important to observe them as people not having the correct papers and stamps will have problems further into either country. At Guyanese immigration (usually closes 1800), have your passport stamped and then go to the police desk

in the same building to be signed in or out. In Brazil, go to Policía Federal on the Brazilian side of the bridge, open 0800-1200, 1400-1800, to get your entry stamp. If you need a visa for Brazil you can apply in Georgetown at the **Brazilian Embassy** ① *308 Church St, Queenstown, T225 7970, http://georgetown.itamaraty.gov.br/ en-us/, Mon-Fri 0900-1400*. But it is advisable to check in advance what requirements are for your nationality. You must have a yellow fever certificate. When entering both Guyana and Brazil, make sure you get a stamp for the number of days you need for your visit. See also Transport, page 56.

The road from Bonfim to Boa Vista is mostly straight, crossing savannah with wet areas and palm trees and wide open fields. The land begins to roll a bit before reaching the bridge over the Rio Branco into Boa Vista.

Listings Guyana *map page 28.*

Tourist information

For details of the **Guyana Tourism Authority**, **Ministry of Business** and the **Tourism and Hospitality Association of Guyana** (THAG), all based in Georgetown, see page 113.

Where to stay

If you plan to stay in Georgetown, it's best to book your lodgings in advance. There isn't much choice in the lower price categories and many small hotels and guesthouses are full of long-stay residents, while some are rented by the hour. If in doubt, go to a larger hotel for the 1st night and look around next day in daylight.

There are several business hotels, near the north shore, eg **$$$-$$ Ocean Spray International** (46 Stanley Pl, Kitty, T227 3763/5, www.oceanspray.co.gy); and **$$$ Atlantic Inn** (56 Church Rd and First Av, Soubryanville, T225 5826, www. atlanticinngy.com), and apartments, eg **$$$$ Blue Wave Apartments** (8 North Rd, Bourda, T226 1418); and **$$$-$$ Brandsville's Apartments** (88-90 Pike St, Campbellville, T227 0989, www.brandsvillegy.com).

Georgetown

$$$$ Cara Lodge
294 Quamina St, T225 5301, http://caralodge.com.
A **Heritage House** hotel, converted 1840s mansion (Woodbine House), with 36 superb rooms, good service, restaurant (see page 46), **Mango Tree Patio** bar, broadband (DSL) internet in rooms, taxi service, laundry, business centre with internet and conference room.

$$$$ Guyana Marriott
Block Alpha, Battery Rd, Kingston, T231 2480, www.marriott.com.
Impressive member of the international chain opened in 2015 with 9 floors and 192 rooms. Excellent amenities.

$$$$ Pegasus Guyana
Seawall Rd, T225 2856, www. pegasushotelguyana.com.
Very safe, a/c, comfortable, fridge, lovely swimming pool, gym, tennis, business centre, massage and yoga, restaurants (**Aromas, El Dorado** serving Italian cuisine and **The Oasis** tea room) and bars (**Ignite, Latino** and **Aura Sky Lounge**). Check internet for special offers. 24-hr back-up electricity.

$$$$ Ramada Georgetown Princess
Providence, East Bank Demerara,
next to Cricket World Cup Stadium,
15-20 mins' drive out of the city,
T265 7009, www.ramada.com.
250 rooms all with a/c, huge pool with
2 pool-side bars, restaurants, including
Providence for international and local
food, **Club Next** and casino.

$$$$-$$$ Duke Lodge
Duke St, Kingston, T227 3807,
http://roraimaairways.com.
Opposite US Embassy, beautiful antique-
style guesthouse 5 mins from central
Georgetown, with breakfast, Wi-Fi,
swimming pool and fine restaurant.

$$$$-$$$ Halito Hotel
176 Middle St, T226 1612/5, Facebook:
Halito Hotel & Residence.
Luxurious, secure, self-contained
rooms with kitchen, grocery, laundry,
internet access, airport pick-up,
restaurant (see page 46).

$$$$-$$$ Roraima Residence Inn
R8 Eping Av, Bel Air Park, T225 9648,
http://roraimaairways.com.
A small hotel with good standards,
a/c and pool.

$$$ El Dorado Inn
295 Thomas and Quamina Streets,
T225 3966, www.eldorado-inn.com.
Good hotel with nicely appointed rooms
in central location. Also has **$$$$** suites.

$$$ Herdmanston Lodge
65 Peter Rose and Anira Streets,
Queenstown, T225 0808, www.
herdmanstonlodge.com.
In a lovely old house, pleasant district,
breakfast, restaurant with daily buffet,
Wi-Fi throughout, very comfortable.

$$$-$$ Grand Coastal Inn
Lot 1 & 2 Area M Plantation,
Le Ressouvenir, 5 km out of city, T220
1091, www.grandcoastal.com.
3 standards of room, with breakfast
and drinking water, dining room, bar,
laundry, business centre with internet,
car rental, tours, good.

$$$-$$ Midtown Hotel
176 Middle St, T623 5011,
www.midtownhotelgy.com/.
Fans and a/c. Includes small breakfast,
also has a **Hibachi** restaurant and bar.
Good, but can be noisy from music and
nightclub next door.

$$$-$$ Millenium Manor
43 Hadfield St, T223 0541,
http://milleniummanor.com.
3 standards of room with all facilities
including **$$$$** suites, modern,
comfortable, helpful staff.

$$$-$$ Tropical View International
33 Delph St, Campbellville, T227 2216/7,
https://tropicalviewinternationalhotel.
shutterfly.com.
Smart, modern hotel in a residential
area, rooms with windows, all mod
cons, Wi-Fi, breakfast included.

$$$-$$ Windjammer International
Cuisine and Comfort Inn
27 Queen St, Kitty, T227 7478,
www.windjammer-gy.com.
30 very comfy rooms in 2 standards, plus
bridal and apartment suites, breakfast
included, a/c, hot water, Créole and West
Indian restaurant, swimming pool.

$$ Sleepin Guesthouse
151 Church St, Alberttown, T223 0991,
www.sleepinguesthouse.com.
A/c, cheaper with fan, some rooms with
kitchenette, Wi-Fi, meals served, also has
car hire. Also **$$$ Sleepin International**,

24 Brickdam, Stabroek, T227 3446,
www.sleepininternationalhotel.com.
Slightly better.

$$ Waterchris
184 Waterloo St, T227 1980,
waterchris@mail.com.
A/c (supposedly), TV, hot water, phone ($
with fan), simple and run-down wooden
rooms, some with shared bath next to a
noisy TV lounge, poor plumbing.

$$-$ Hotel Glow
23 Queen St, Kitty, T227 0863.
Clean, a/c or fan, some with TV, 24-hr
Amigo restaurant, breakfast extra, taxi
or minibus to centre.

$$-$ Melbourne Inn
29B Sheriff St, Campbellville, T226 7050,
sattie_naraine@yahoo.com.
On this famous street, rooms with and
without a/c, some with kitchen, all with
bath, car hire.

$ Rima Guest House
92 Middle St, T225 7401,
rima@networksgy.com.
Good central area, well run, modern,
popular with backpackers, no a/c, hot,
communal bath and toilets, good value,
internet, safe, mosquito nets, restaurant
(breakfast US$6, lunch/dinner US$8).
Mrs Nellie Singh is very helpful. Highly
recommended, book ahead.

Resorts near Georgetown

$$$$ Arrowpoint Nature Resort
Contact at R8 Eping Av, Bel Air Park,
Georgetown, T225 9648, or 94-95 Duke
St, Kingston, Georgetown, T231 7220,
www.roraimaairways.com, Facebook:
ArrowPointResort.
In the heart of the Santa Mission
Amerindian reservation, offers a
"back to nature experience", excellent

birdwatching, with numerous other
activities such as mountain biking and
canoeing. Transport, meals and activities
are all included in the price. Reserve
through **Roraima Airways** or tour
operators (see page 50).

$$ Pandama Retreat and Winery
Plot 9 Madewini, Soesdyke/Linden
Highway (just before Splashmin's
Fun Park), T654 1865/627 7063,
www.pandamaretreat.com.
Tucked away in sand forest along the
Madewini Creek, good for relaxation,
offers a wide range of programmes
with a spiritual, educational and artistic
focus, aimed at small groups. Breakfast
included. Produces quality wines from
local fruit. Day visit US$5, camping
US$15, cabins US$50, meals US$7.50-10.

New Amsterdam and the Berbice river

$$ Church View Guest House
3 Main St and King St, T333 2880,
churchviewhotel@networksgy.com.
Breakfast extra, room rate includes 1 hr
in gym, a/c, cheaper without, phone,
TV, Wi-Fi.

$$$-$$ Little Rock Suites
10 Main St and Church St, T333 2727,
littlerocksuitesgy@yahoo.com.
Central, rooms of various sizes, a/c, fridge,
with restaurant and **Wine Tavern** and
Eclipse Bar.

$$ Parkway
4 Main St, T333 6438.
Clean, a/c, safe, with bath, breakfast,
lunch and dinner extra. Recommended.

Berbice resorts

$$ pp Dubulay Ranch
A working ranch on the Berbice river,
147 km from the river mouth, has

forest, savannah and swamp habitats, with some 300 bird species, deer, large cats, water buffalo and Dutch colonial remains. Activities include boat trips, riding, birdwatching, jeep tours, night-time wildlife trips, custom-made packages, or just relaxing. Cheaper rates for scientists or students, includes 3 meals and soft drinks/juices, but not transport to the ranch (US$230 return from/to Georgetown) or activities. Small parties preferred; advance booking essential. Can be booked through any tour operator.

Corriverton

$$ Mahogany
50 Public Rd, Springlands, T335 3525, vicgreene72@yahoo.com.
With bath, TV, fridge, hot water, clean, lunch/dinner available. Recommended.

Others include **$$ Malinmar** (13 Public Rd, Springlands, T333 3328, sandramuniram@yahoo.com), **$$ Riverton Suites** (Lot 78 Springlands, T335 3039, hotelriverton@hotmail.com), and **$ Paraton Inn** (K & L 78, Corriverton, T339 2413).

West from Georgetown:
Lake Mainstay

In Charity are **Hotel Purple Heart, Restaurant and Bar** (103-104 Charity, *T771 5209, hotelpurpleheart@yahoo.com*), and **Xenon** (*190 Charity, T771 4989/629 6231*).

$$$-$$ Lake Mainstay Resort
T226 2975, http://lakemainstayonline.com.
40 cabins with a/c, cheaper without lake view, also single rooms, beachfront on the lake, **Horoshi Restaurant**, bars, swimming, boating, other sports, birdwatching and nature trails, entertainment. All meals available and various all-inclusive

packages for 2 to 3 days. The resort can arrange road and boat transport, otherwise go with own transport.

Adel's Rainforest Resort
Akawinni Creek, Pomeroon river, T771 5391/696 0574, www.adelresort.com.
In a pristine location 3 hrs from Georgetown, ideal for relaxation and tours of the Pomeroon river and Akawinni Creek, fishing, etc. All-inclusive accommodation with fruit and veg from organic garden; other local produce available.

Border with Venezuela: Mabaruma

$ Regional Guest House
T777 5091.
2 rooms with bath or shared bath, clean, book in advance.

$ Kumaka Tourist Resort
Maburama, contact Somwaru Travel Agency, 35 North Rd, Lacytown, Georgetown, T225 9276, or 777 5140, somwarutravelgy@ymail.com.
Meals, bath; offers trips to Hosororo Falls, Babarima Amerindian settlement, rainforest, early examples of Amerindian art.

Bartica

$$$-$ Platinum Inn International
Lot 7, First Av, T455 3041.
Range of rooms from suite with a/c, cable TV and fridge, to fan and TV, weekend packages available, internet, tours arranged, restaurant and bar.

$$-$ The New Modern Hotel & Nightclub
9 First Av, T455 2301, near ferry.
2 standards of room, with bath and fan. Recommended. Good food, best to book ahead.

Resorts near Bartica

$$$$-$$$ Baganara Island Resort
Beautiful house on Baganara Island in Essequibo river a few miles south of Bartica, T222 8053, http://baganara.net.
Price depends on season and standard of room, full board, private beach, watersports, airstrip; day trips US$85 pp (minimum 12), includes road and boat transport, snacks, lunch, local soft drinks, VAT, activities and guide. Transport to resort from Bartica US$30 pp return.

$$$$-$$$ Hurakabra River Resort
On the west bank of the Essequibo, 5 km from Bartica, about 2 hrs from Georgetown, booking office 1687 Century Palm Gardens, Durban Backlands, Lodge, T226 0240, www.hurakabra.com.
This nature resort has a choice of 2 lodgings, the grand **Mango Tree Villa**, which can sleep 8-10, and **Bamboo Cottage**, for 2 people, both on the waterfront with tropical forest behind, bamboo groves, mango trees and abundant birdlife, many activities included in price, arranges local tours.

Sloth Island Nature Reserve
5 mins by boat from Bartica, T227 5575, www.slothisland.com.
On a forested island with good birdwatching and other wildlife, large, fan-cooled rooms, also hammocks, restaurant, bar, excursions.

Kaieteur National Park

The (**$**) guesthouse near the top of the falls is basic; it has beds with mosquito nets, hammocks, a kitchen, toilet and cold shower. Enquire and pay first at the **National Parks Commission** (Georgetown, T225 9142). If planning to stay overnight, you must be self-sufficient, whether the guesthouse is open or not; take your own food (and a hammock if the guesthouse is closed), it can be cold and damp at night; the warden is not allowed to collect money. The guesthouse is 15 mins' walk from the airstrip. The park office sells drinks and sweets – nothing else.

Linden

As well as those listed below you can try the **$$ Crimson Bat** (633 Industrial Area, Mackenzie, T444 2102), primarily a restaurant and disco; **$$ Massive Inn** (Fraser Rd, Kara Kara, Mackenzie, T444 6383); **$ Summit Hotel** (6 Industrial Area, McKenzie, T444 6500); **$$ The Linden Guest House** (Lot 331 Greenheart St, Mackenzie, T444 3147, contact through Durban Hotel, 7 Durban St, Georgetown, T227 5890, www.thedurbanhotel.com).

$$ Barrow's
82 Dageraad and Manni St, Mackenzie, T444 6799, dunbarr@ networksgy.com.
All double/twin, hot water, a/c, TV, fridge, popular restaurant and bar below.

$$ Watooka Guesthouse
130 Riverside Drive, Watooka, T444 2162, watookacomplex@yahoo.com.
In a historic building, old British charm with a tropical flavour, comfortable a/c rooms on ground and 1st floors, swimming pool, restaurant and bar.

$$-$ Morning Star: Star Bonnett Restaurant & Hotel
671 Industrial Area, 1.5 km out of town on Georgetown Rd, T444 6505, morningstar671industiralarea@ gmail.com, see Facebook.
Various standards of room, all with a/c and TV, clean, breakfast US$4, good lunches (US$6-12.50).

Iwokrama

There are places to stay at each end of the Iwokrama reserve, used mainly by bus passengers on the Georgetown-Lethem routes. At the northern entrance is **Charlie's Rainforest Lodge** and at the southern end, at the Surama road junction, is **Madonna's**. At each you can hire a hammock in a benab for US$2.55, or a simple room with fan for US$25 (Charlie's) or US$21 (Madonna's, which also serves meals, including vegetarian, has a shop and electricity). Guests stay for a few hours' rest on the journey and leave in time to catch the first ferry across the Essequibo.

Note Wi-Fi is available in most of the lodges in Iwokrama and the Rupununi, but it is supplied on a monthly basis by satellite and solar power and use for guests is strictly limited. Follow instructions given to you by the staff and do not up- or download pictures or indulge in any other bandwidth-sapping activities. If you overuse the system the lodge will be without Wi-Fi until the next month.

$$$$ pp Atta Rainforest Lodge
http://iwokramacanopywalkway.com (booking office 141 4th St, Georgetown, T227 7698, Wilderness Explorers.
For visits to the Iwokrama Canopy Walkway, 8 rooms with bath, with a bar, dining area and Wi-Fi, US$5 per hr. Mosquito nets provided, comfortable beds, good bathrooms. Restaurant serves breakfast, lunch and dinner, excellent food (US$15, 20 and 25 respectively if not staying at the lodge). The overnight trip rate includes entry to the **Iwokrama Canopy Walkway**, trained guide, 3 meals. Visitors can experience the dawn chorus and be on the walkway at dusk and into the night.

They have many short and extended trails. Birds include crimson fruitcrow, white-winged potoo and a family of black curassow that regularly feed in the lodge's gardens. Night-time jaguar-spotting trips on a motorbike-drawn trailer with bench seats are an option.

$$$$ Iwokrama River Lodge
77 High St, Kingston, Georgetown, PO Box 10630, T225 1504, http://iwokrama. org and http://iwokramariverlodge.com.
The River Lodge is one of the most comfortable in South America in a beautiful setting on the banks of the Essequibo, next to pristine forest, full of giant moura trees and kapoks. It has 2 types of accommodation, in 8 free-standing cabins or in rooms in the research building (**$$** or **$** per person). The cabins are comfortable, with bath and veranda. Meals are served in huge dining research area with a library and bar which offers alcoholic beverages at extra cost; breakfast US$8, lunch US$12, dinner US$15. 2-day/1-night packages are available from US$379-608 per person; price depends on the number of activities included.

$ Michelle's Island
On the Georgetown side of the Essequibo ferry crossing, T639 5716.
Michelle has a bar serving food and drinks and she also owns an island bearing her name in the river where you can stay in cabins if you want to break the journey, arranges boat trips.

Surama

See page 35, above.

Rupununi Savannah

The following can be booked independently online or by phone. Because of limited communication and

the shortage of scheduled flights, it may be helpful to engage a tour operator to arrange all transport.

Annai

$$$$ The Rock View Lodge
Between Annai and Rupertee, http://rockviewlodge.com.
This relaxing, comfortable lodge has 8 self-contained rooms, price includes all meals, all drinks, hot water, fans, Wi-Fi, laundry and guided tours (horse riding is extra). Room only is **$$$** but Wi-Fi and meals can be paid for separately (breakfast US$10, lunch US$15, dinner US$25 without drinks). There is a natural rock swimming pool and a lookout point on a rock in attractive gardens. The lodge is family owned and operated. The Edwards are a blend of Amerindian, Brazilian, British and Basque who are proud to represent the heritage, skills, local knowledge and personalities that make up Guyana's brand of tourism. Activities include nature tours for painting, photography and birding, regional Amerindian and other local cooking, culture and agrotourism. Recommended. Transport can be arranged to/from the Georgetown–Lethem road and Surama.

Lodges in the Rupunini

$$$$ pp Dadanawa Ranch
Duane and Sandy de Freitas, 96 km south of Lethem, one of the world's largest ranches, each bedroom has a verandah (being upgraded).
Their tour operator, **Rupununi Trails** (T+44-796-152 1951, www.rupununitrails.com), can organize trekking, birding, horse riding and fishing trips, rainforest adventures and camping with *vaqueros*. One of the most

spectacular wildlife destinations in South America. Very remote and expensive but a high chance of seeing big cats, other large mammals and the harpy eagle.

$$$$ pp Karanambu Lodge
On the Rupununi river, www.karanambutrustandlodge.org/.
96 km northeast of Lethem, unique old home, 5 cottages with bath (1 suitable for a family) around a large compound with flowers and mango trees, mosquito net, toiletries, good meals, solar energy, small shop selling local handicrafts, fishing, excellent birdwatching and boat rides with guides, including to see Victoria Amazonica flowers which open at dusk, daily giant-anteater spotting trip. Wi-Fi, bar and camping area due to be installed. 24 km from Yupukari Amerindian village, trips possible. For many years Dianne McTurk reared and rehabilitated orphaned giant river otters, and, thanks to her, the population on the river is now healthy, with otters spreading to other rivers. There are no otters in residence at Karanambu (2016) and, sadly, Dianne McTurk died in late 2016. The lodge is now run by her relatives, Jerry and Melanie McTurk, and they have plans to create a sanctuary for rescued wildlife and run other projects to improve human conditions and thus relieve stress on the savannah's wild environment.

$$$ pp Caiman House Field Station
At Yupukari village on the Rupununi river, www.rupununilearners.org.
A centre principally for black caiman, but also giant river turtle research, plus projects with the community, such as public library and furniture making. The field station has a guesthouse with simple rooms in 2 buildings, the majority en suite, local furniture, simple bathrooms. It also has hammock space

for US$60 per day. All prices include 3 meals a day, good local food. Guests can go on and participate (in a minor way) in night research trips, walk local trails, go birdwatching and on boat trips and get to know the Yupukari community. All transport and activities cost extra.

$$$$ Rewa Eco-Lodge
Rewa Village, on the Rupununi river at its junction with the Rewa river, contact through the website, http:// rewaecolodge.com.
This lodge is 2-3 hrs by boat from Kwatamang Landing, or by boat from Apoteri, which has an airstrip. It is run by the Rewa community and visitors are encouraged to visit the nearby village. 4 bedrooms in 2 *benabs* (shelters) with shared bath and toilets; 4 cabins with en suite facilities (3 more under construction in 2016); 1 *benab* with dining room; hammocks, solar lighting. Quietly efficient, immaculately kept, good food. Packages include sport fishing in Bat Creek, harpy eagle or wild cats viewing (best Nov-Apr), arapaima spotting at Grass Pond oxbow lake, excellent birdwatching, trek up Awarmie Mountain (900 m, best in the early morning). 2- and 3-night packages available; price varies according to number of guests and how many activities are to be included.

Lethem

$$$ Maipaima Eco-Lodge
56 km from Lethem in Nappi village, Kanuku Mountains, T772 2085, http://maipaimaecolodge.com.
Community-run lodge with plenty of wildlife-viewing opportunities, hikes in rainforest and to waterfalls. One of the best activities is the hike to Jordon Falls

where you can camp, 4-6 hrs through pristine forest to a waterfall. 2 cabins (with more being built) and a large dining hall, each cabin sleeps up to 8, buildings are elevated and connected by walkways. Hammock accommodation **$**.

$$$ Manari Ranch
20 mins' drive north of Lethem on Manari Creek, T668 2006, Facebook: manariranch, or contact through Wilderness Explorers (page 50).
Great atmosphere, comfortable rooms and good food, savannah treks, drifts down river and out into the Ireng river, bird- and wildlife watching provided.

$$$ Ori Hotel and Restaurant
118 Lethem, T772 2124, http://origuyana.com.
Self-contained cabins and rooms with Wi-Fi, also has a guesthouse, fridge, restaurant and bar, excellent view of mountains from upper balcony, changes reais to Guyana dollars.

$$$-$$ Rupununi Eco Hotel
51-53 Commercial Area, T623 3060 (Daniel), 644 3201 (Michelle), http:// www.rupununiecohotel.com.
Economy, standard and luxury rooms, with breakfast and Wi-Fi, all with a/c, microwave, fridge, luxury rooms have better bathrooms and carpet. More rooms and swimming pool being built (2106).

$ pp Savannah Inn
T772 2035 (Georgetown T227 4938), www.savannahguyana.com.
Including breakfast, a/c cabins and rooms with bath, fridge, benab with hammocks, garden, dining room with free fruit, juice and hot drinks, changes reais into Guyanese dollars, tours arranged, will pick you up from airport or border with prior notice. Advance bookings only.

$ Takutu
430 Lethem, T772 2034.
Simple a/c and fan-cooled rooms, also hammock space, US$5, good value, fridge, clean, all meals extra.

Camps

$$$ Maparri Wilderness Camp
Contact Wilderness Explorers (page 50) for rates and bookings. It can only be reached by air and river. See also www.rupununitrails.com.
On the Maparri river, in the Kanuku mountains (see page 37), it is easy to watch macaws, herons, toucans, kingfishers, maybe harpy eagles from this camp. With luck, you can see tayra, labba, ocelot, agouti, monkeys, tapir and even jaguar. Various treks are arranged. Built of wood, with open sides, it has hammocks with mosquito nets. The site overlooks a waterfall; the river water is crystal clear (unlike most rivers in Guyana) and the fall and surrounding pools are safe for swimming. Simple, nutritional meals, and fish from the river, are prepared over an open fire.

Restaurants

Georgetown
A 10% service may be added to the bill. Many restaurants are closed on public holidays. Restaurants are categorized according to their most expensive dishes. All have much cheaper options on the menus.

Sheriff St is some way east of the centre but is 'the street that never sleeps' full of late-night Chinese restaurants, eg **Buddy's Mei Tung Restaurant** (No 137, T231 4100), very good, with nightclub and pool hall, and has some good bars including **Club Monaco** (No 63A, T223 3915) and **Royal Castle**

(No 52 at Garnett St), for chicken burgers. Also **Aagman's** (No 28-A, T219 0161) and **Maharaja Palace** (No 207, T219 4346), serve Indian food; while **Antonio's Grille** (No 172 and 5th St, T225 7933) serves both international and local cuisine and **Kamboat** (No 51, T225 8323, delivery T225 8090) is recommended for Chinese.

$$$ Bistro 176
At Halito Hotel, see page 39.
Restaurant and bar offering local and international cuisine.

$$$ Bottle Bar and Restaurant at Cara Lodge
Very good, pleasant surroundings, must book, also open for breakfast.

$$$ Café Tepuy
R 8 Eping Av, Bel Air Park, T225 9648.
Serves both international and local cuisine.

$$$ Golden Coast
62 Main St and Middle St, T231 7360.
Chinese, good food, huge portions, classy.

$$$ Gravity Lounge
United Center Mall, Camp St and Regent St, T226 8858.
Top-end restaurant and VIP lounge on the 6th floor, panoramic views, popular at weekends, often has Caribbean artistes.

$$$ The New Palm Court
35 Main St, T231 8144, Facebook: palmcourtgy. Open 1100-0200.
Bar and restaurant with international and vegetarian food as well as drinks.

$$$ Play Land
American Italiano Family Restaurant, Lot 70, Park St, Enterprise, East Coast Demerara, T229 7100, http:// playlanditaliano.net.
Out of town, but a good place to enjoy Italian food in a Guyanese setting.

$$$-$$ Lily's
87C Barrack St, T231 9804,
lilysfastfoodcafe@gmail.com.
A whole range of different dishes,
from breakfast to traditional, Cajun/
Creole, Caribbean, Asian, burgers
and sandwiches.

$$$-$$ Tuma Sàlà
249 BB Eccles EBD, T663 2818, Facebook:
Tuma Sàlà. Open 0800-2000.
Specializing in Amerindian dishes,
including fish, wild meat, cassava bread,
vegetables, fruit, juices and indigenous
wines and teas. Also has a craft shop.

$$$-$$ Xie Xie
159A West Barr St and Alexander St,
T225 7769, Facebook: xiexiecafe.
High-quality food with a great
atmosphere, daily lunch specials
Mon-Sat from 1130.

$$$-$ Coalpot
Camp St, between Quamina St and
Church St.
Good lunches starting at US$1.80,
up to US$13.15 (no shorts allowed,
cheaper *cafetería*).

$$$-$ New Thriving
Main St, the building before Customs
House, T225 0038.
A/c, buffet restaurant with large,
oily portions.

$$ Brazil Churrascaria
208 Alexander St, Lacytown, T225 6037.
All you can eat for US$15. Great food.

$$ Church's Chicken
Camp St and Middle St, T225 7546.
For chicken and fries.

$$ The Coffee Bean Café and Eatery
133 Church St, South Cummingsburg,
T223 2222, Facebook:coffeebean.gy.

For coffees, teas, juices, pastries,
breakfasts and lunches of wraps,
sandwiches and pastas.

$$ Hibiscus Restaurant and Lounge
91 Middle St, T231 5866, Facebook:
HibiscusRestaurantLounge.
Typical sports bar, varied Western menu,
outdoor area, popular hang-out bar.

$$ JR Burgers
3 Sandy Babb St, Kitty, T226 6614.
Popular. Also in the City Mall. In the
same building is **Silhouette** restaurant
and **Altitude Lounge and Bar**, on
3rd floor, same phone, a cocktail bar
serving local food. Also a drive-through
section next door.

$$ Mario's Pizza
Camp St and Middle St, T231 2639.
Opposite **Church's Chicken**. Variety
of pizza.

$$ Popeye's
1e Vissengen Rd and Duncan St,
T223 6226.
Serves chicken.

$$ White Castle Fish Shop
21 Hadfield and John St, Werk-en-rust,
T223 0921.
Casual open-air bar, for great fried fish
and chips. Delivery available.

$$-$ German's
8 New Market St, North Cummingsburg,
T227 0079.
Creole food with an emphasis on its
traditional soups.

$$-$ Hacks Halaal
5 Commerce St, T226 1844.
Specializes in Creole foods and snacks,
local juices.

$$-$ Rayman's Halaal
11-14 Lombard and Princess St, T225 0399.
Halaal restaurant and sweetmeat shop.

$$-$ Shanta's
The Puri Shop, 225 Camp and New Market St, Cummingsburg, T226 4365.
Local cuisine, a wide variety of Indian and African dishes, casual in-house dining or take-away.

$ Oasis Café
125 Carmichael St, South Cummingsburg, T226 9916, www.oasiscafegy.com.
Fashionable and safe, has Wi-Fi access. Serves Creole food, mainly lunch, and has a Fri evening restaurant, **Oasis Paradiso**, T681 1648 for reservations, open 1930-2300 Probably the best coffee in Georgetown. Recommended. Also **Oasis Express** at the Cheddi Jagan International Airport, T261 3016. Sandwiches, snacks, drinks, etc.

$ Upscale
Regent St and Hinck St, T225 4721.
Popular, poetry night Tue, comedy night Fri.

Cafés

Juice Power
Middle St, past the hospital.
Excellent fruit juices, also sells drinking water.

Maggie's Snackette
224 New Market St, Cummingsburg, T226 2226.
Authentic Guyanese food, cakes, pastries and fruit drinks, very popular.

Quizno's
Camp St and Middle St, T225 1527.
Lunches, sandwiches, salads and soups.

Rupununi Savannah
Annai

The Oasis
On the Lethem–Georgetown road, T644 8101, ask for William.

Bar and *churrascaria* restaurant serving Brazilian and Guyanese food, shop (used to be part of **Rock View** with economical accommodation, but sleeping facilities have been taken back to Rock View). Interesting nature trail in front of the Oasis up a forest-covered hill – sweeping views of the savannah – channel-billed toucans very common.

Lethem
There are a number of eating places, including at hotels and guesthouses. Several sell Brazilian-influenced dishes.
By the airport are **Shirley & Sons**, which is a gift shop and bar, and **Touch Down Bar & Lounge**.

Betty's Creole Corner
At a crossroads behind Savannah Inn.
Local food, snacks, juices and shop.

Bars and clubs

Georgetown
There are a number of modern bars, clubs and lounges hosting a variety of parties most nights, popular with Georgetown residents and Guyanese from outside the city. Most nightclubs sell imported, as well as local Banks beer. Don't walk home at night; take a taxi. See under Restaurants, above, for Sheriff St.

704 Sports Bar
Lamaha St and Albert St, Queenstown, T225 0252.
Sports, entertainment and food, also has a night club and **Sky Lounge** on different floors of the building.

> **Tip...**
> Many places sell drinks by the bottle rather than shot, which works out cheaper.

The 592 Hub
177 Waterloo St, T227 5701.
With performing arts.

The Vintage Wine and Cheese Lounge
218 Lamaha and Camp St, T231 9631.
Wine and cheese bar with other meals and drinks.

Entertainment

Cinema
2 cinemas also at the **Fun City Arcade** at the **Princess Hotel** (see Ramada Georgetown Princess, page 39, T265 7212, princessfuncity@yahoo.com). The Arcade has more than 80 games.

Theatre
There are 2 theatres.

Shopping

Georgetown
The main shopping area is Regent St.

Crafts
Items that are a good buy: Amerindian basketwork, hammocks, wood carvings, pottery, and small figures made out of *balata*, a rubbery substance tapped from trees in the interior. Look for such items in the markets (also T-shirts), or craft shops. **Creations Craft** (Water St); **Amerindian Hostel** (Princess St), **Hibiscus Craft Plaza** (outside General Post Office). Others are advertised in the papers.

Department stores and other shops
Fogarty's and **Guyana Stores** (Church St), both stock a wide range of goods (good T-shirts at the latter).
City Mall, *Regent St and Camp St, T225 6644.* Is a small mall with everything from food to jewellers.

Footsteps Mega Store, *141 Camp St and Regent St, in the United Center Mall.* For a wide range of goods, from clothing to furniture and household items (also at Camp St and Charlotte St and America St and Longden St).
Giftland Mall, *in Turkeyen.* The largest mall in Guyana with 120 concessions, 8 cinemas, restaurants and the largest department store in the Caribbean.
Georgetown Reading and Research Centre, *Woolford Av, in the Critchlow Labour College.* A wide range of books, used and new, at really great prices.

Gold
Gold is sold widely, often at good prices but make sure you know what you are buying. Do not buy it on the street.

Markets
Most Guyanese do their regular shopping at the 4 big markets: **Stabroek** (don't take valuables), **Bourda**, **La Penitence** and **Kitty**.

What to do

Georgetown
The tourism sector is promoting ecotourism in the form of environmentally friendly resorts and camps on Guyana's rivers and in the rainforest. There is much tropical wildlife to be seen. Tours to Amerindian villages close to Georgetown cost US$95-160.

Tour operators
Dagron Tours, *91 Middle St, T223 7921, www.dagron-tours.com.* Well-established company offering adventure and eco-tours within Guyana, including to the Rupununi, to resorts near Bartica, Kaieteur and Orinduik; programmes to the 3 Guianas; tours to Brazil, Venezuela

and the Caribbean. Also offer day tours, birdwatching and student field trips.

Evergreen Adventures, *Ogle Aerodrome, Ogle, East Coast Demerara, T222 8053, www.evergreenadventuresgy.com.* Tours on the Essequibo river to Baganara Island, plus bookings for other lodges and tours. Sister company to **Trans Guyana Airways**.

Old Fort Tours, *91 Middle St, T260 4536, www.angcamgy.com/old-fort-fours [sic].* Tours of Georgetown, Kaieteur, Shell Beach, road and river trips throughout the country.

Rainforest Tours, *5 Av of the Republic and Robb St, T231 5661, www.rftours.com.* Frank Singh, day and overland trips to Kaieteur, Santa Mission, Essequibo/Mazaruni; also Pakaraima Mountain trip, Kukubara to Orinduik, 5 days from one Amerindian village to another.

Roraima Airways, *R8 Eping Av, Bel Air Park, T225 9647, www.roraimaairways.com.* Day trips to Kaieteur and Arrowpoint.

Splashmin's, *48 High St, Werk-en-rust, Georgetown, T223 7301, www.splashmins. com.* A water park on the Linden highway, 1 hr from the city, entrance and transportation from Georgetown: adult US$5.10, child US$2.55, children 4 and under free. Also has a resort ($$$) and camping grounds.

Torong Guyana, *56 Coralita Av, Bel Air Park, T225 0876/226 5298, toronggy@ networksgy.com.* Air, land and river advice and logistical support to all destinations in Guyana, bespoke tours country-wide and excellent trips to Kaieteur.

Wilderness Explorers, *141 Fourth St, Campbellville, T227 7698, www. wilderness-explorers.com. (In London: c/o Claire Antell, 46 Melbourne Rd, London SW19 3BA, T020-8417 1585.)* Offer ready-made or custom-designed itineraries. Tours to all of Guyana's interior resorts, day and overland tours to Kaieteur Falls, horse trekking, hiking and general tours in the Rupununi (agents for **Ranches of the Rupununi**) and rainforest (trips to **Iwokrama Rainforest Programme** and joint managers of **Iwokrama Canopy Walkway**, see page 35). Tours also in Suriname, Guyane, Brazil, Venezuela, Barbados, Dominica, St Lucia and Trinidad and Tobago. Specialists in nature, adventure and birdwatching tours. Self-drive 4WD adventures in combination with **Europcar** (see below and page 74 under Paramaribo),

14 days from US$5565 including all lodges, meals, drinks, excursions and activities as well as the vehicle (can drop vehicle in Lethem and fly back to Georgetown); driver/guide can also be provided. Free tourism information, booklet and advice available. General sales agents for **Air Services Ltd** and **Trans Guyana Airways**. Representatives: North America: T202-630 7689. Europe: Claudia Langer, claudia@wilderness-explorers.com.

Wonderland Tours, *85 Quamina St and Carmichael St, T225 3122, www. wonderlandtoursgy.com*. Day trips to Kaieteur and Orinduik Falls, Santa Mission, Essequibo and Mazaruni rivers, city tours; special arrangements for overnight stays available, recommended.

Travel agents

Connections Travel, *6 Av of the Republic.*
Frandec, *126 Quamaina St and Carmichael St, opposite Beacon Snackette, T226 3076, www.frandec.com*. Mr Mendoza. Repeatedly recommended (no tours to the interior).
Muneshwers Ltd, *45-47 Water St.*
Survival, *173 Sheriff St, Campbellville, T227 8506, survivaltravelagency@ networksgy.com.*

New Amsterdam and the Berbice river

Cortours, *33 Grant, 1651 Crabwood Creek, Berbice, T335 0853/339 2430, cortoursinc@ yahoo.com*. Offers package tours to Orealla village, Cow Falls and Wanatoba Falls for overnight visits and peacock bass fishing.

Bartica

B Balkarran, *2 Triangle St, T455 2544.* A good boatman and guide.
Essequibo Adventure Tours, *52 First Av, T455 2441, sbell@guyananet.gy*. Jet boat and tours on the Essequibo/Mazaruni and Cuyuni rivers.

Lethem

Bushmasters Ltd, *Rupununi Whistler, T682 4175, www.bushmasters.co.uk*. Adventure tours, safaris and survival courses, Guyanese guides and British staff.

Georgetown

Minibuses run regularly to most parts of the city, mostly from Stabroek market or Av of the Republic. Collective taxis ply set routes at a fixed fare; they stop at any point on request. Taxis can be taken within and outside the city limits.

Air

Cheddi Jagan International Airport, www.cjairport-gy.com, is at Timehri, 40 km south of Georgetown (a new Arrivals terminal is being built and there are plans to expand the runway). From the airport, take minibus No 42 to Georgetown US$2, 1-1½ hrs (from Georgetown it leaves from next to the Parliament building); for a small charge they will take you to your hotel (similarly for groups going to the airport). A taxi costs from US$25 (use approved airport taxis, T261 2281). Check in 3 hrs before most flights and contact the airline the day before your flight to hear if it has been delayed, or brought forward. Check-in queues can be long and the terminal overcrowded if several flights are scheduled for the same time. There is 1 small canteen and 3 duty-free shops. Some spirits are more expensive than downtown. There is also an exchange house, open usual banking hrs; if closed, there are plenty of parallel traders outside (signboard in the exchange house says what the rate is). It is difficult to pay for flight tickets at the airport with credit cards.

    Ogle International Airport, www. ogleairportguyana.com, for internal flights, **LIAT** international flights and most flights to **Suriname**, has an extended runway and new immigration and customs facilities. It is 15 mins from

Georgetown; taxi US$7.50-10, minibus from Market to Ogle US$0.50. (**Suriname Airways** also have flights to Suriname on Tue and Sat from Cheddi Jagan.)

Flights are often booked up weeks in advance (especially at Christmas and in Aug) and are frequently overbooked, so it is essential to reconfirm an outward flight within 72 hrs of arrival, which can take some time, and it is difficult to change your travel plans at the last minute. A number of travel agents are now computerized, making the process easier. Check for special deals on flights to neighbouring countries. Foreigners must pay for airline tickets in US$ (most airlines do not accept US$100 bills), or other specified currencies. Luggage should be securely locked as theft from checked-in baggage is common.

For information on how to get to Guyana see Getting there, page 103, and for domestic flights see Getting around, page 105.

Bus
Within the city, minibuses run regularly to most parts, mostly from Stabroek market or Av of the Republic, fare G$80-140 (US$0.40-0.70, depending on destination) very crowded. It is difficult to get a seat during rush hours. There are regular services by minibuses and collective taxis to most coastal towns from the Stabroek market. Minibuses leave early; arrive before 0700. To **Rosignol**, No 50, US$2; to **Parika**, No 32, US$2.50; to **Linden**, No 43, US$5. Ask other passengers what the fare is.

Car hire
Car hire is available through numerous companies (the Guyana telephone book lists some of them and the rest can be found in the Yellow Pages). **Europcar**,

141 Fourth St, Campbellville, T225 1019/623 0495, www.europcar.com. Rent 4WD and SUVs (see above under **Wilderness Explorers**, page 50, for fly/drive packages). **Shivraj**, 98 Hadfield St, Werk-en-Rust, T226 0550/225 4785, carl@solution.com. US$54.65 plus US$220 deposit.

Taxi
Taxis charge US$2 for short journeys, US$5 for longer runs, with higher rates at night (a safe option) and outside the city limits. Collective taxis ply set routes at a fixed fare; they stop at any point on request. Certain hand signals are used on some routes to indicate the final destination (ask). Special taxis at hotels and airports, marked 'special' on the windscreen, charge about a third more than regular taxis, or you can negotiate a 'by the hour' deal.

Southeast to Suriname
Boat
To **Suriname** A ferry from Moleson, or Crabwood Creek, 13 km south of Springlands, to **South Drain** (40 km south of Nieuw-Nickerie, paved road) the **Canawaima**, T339 2744, runs once or twice daily depending on demand, at 0900 and 1300 (1100 if once a day), check-in 0630-0800 and 1030-1200, US$10 single (US$15 return for 21 days), bicycles free, motorbikes US$5, cars US$30, pick-ups US$40, 30-min crossing. Immigration forms are handed out on board. At the ferry point is a hut/bar where you can buy Suriname dollars.

Bus
To Moleson Creek from the capital for the crossing to **Suriname**, No 63 from opposite Georgetown City Hall, Av of the Republic between Regent

St and Charlotte St, leaves when full, US$12.75. This is not a safe area early in the morning, if there are no other passengers waiting take a taxi to Moleson Creek from Georgetown, US$125. **Champ Bus & Taxi Service**, T629 6735, runs taxi service to **Moleson Creek** and a bus to **Paramaribo**. If, by mistake, you get on a bus going only as far as **Springlands**, US$10.25, 15 mins before Moleson Creek, 3-4 hrs, the driver will probably take you for a little extra money (check with the driver in Georgetown where his bus is going); you can also break the journey at New Amsterdam. Entering Guyana, you may be able to join a Paramaribo–Georgetown minibus at Immigration. You have to change buses once across the border; you are given a card to hand to the bus driver in the next country. Direct buses Georgetown–Paramaribo are operated by **Dougla**, T226 2843; they pick up and drop off at hotels. Minibuses to Paramaribo by **Bobby's**, T226 8668, **Lambada, Bin Laden**, T264 2993/624 2411, and **Champ** (see above). Fares are US$50-60, not including the ferry crossing; they pick up and drop off at hotels. Check visa requirements for Suriname before travelling.

Border with Venezuela: Mabaruma
Air
ASL flies from Georgetown daily at 0700, return 0800 (in Mabaruma T664 2940/777 5003).

Boat
A ferry runs every other Tue from Georgetown at 1500 (US$8.35) to **Mabaruma**. The journey is surprisingly rough and "you will have to fight for hammock space and watch your possessions like a hawk". For assistance with transport contact Mr Prince through the **Government Guest House**. Boats also go from **Charity** (see page 32) when there is demand. Ask for Peanut or Gavin. Boats go out to sea so you will get very wet and it can be rough, 6 hrs, costs up to US$100 per boat.

Shell Beach
Air/boat
Fly Georgetown–**Mabaruma**, then take a motorized canoe to **Shell Beach**, 1 hr (good trip in the early morning for birdwatching); lasting 20 mins, it goes from the mouth of the Waini river along coast to Shell Beach camp, which can be a jolting ride. An alternative route crosses the Demerara and Essequibo rivers, continuing to Charity then taking various boat rides on the Pomeroon and Waina rivers to the Atlantic. Allow 3-4 days. Contact **Wilderness Explorers** and other Georgetown operators, see page 50. Note that tours to Shell Beach were not running in 2017 owing to flooding.

Bartica
Air
Flight from Ogle to **Bartica** with **TGA** Wed, Fri 0700, 1600, Sun 1600, return 30 mins later (in Bartica T600 9100). The morning flight lands at Baganara only, with a boat connection to Bartica; the afternoon flight lands at Bartica only, with a boat to Baganara if there are passengers to or from Baganara.

Kaieteur and Orinduik Falls
Organized tours
A trip to the **Kaieteur Falls** alone costs US$220-260 with most operators, minimum 5, 8 or 12 people, depending on the aircraft. The other most popular day trip includes 2 hrs at Kaieteur Falls, lunch, drinks, park entrance fee and

guide, plus 2 hrs at Orinduik Falls for US$260-290; take swimming gear. Trips depend on the charter plane being filled; there is normally at least 1 flight per week. Cancellations only occur in bad weather or if there are insufficient passengers. Operators offering this service are **Wilderness Explorers** (guarantees flight to Kaieteur Falls for flights booked as part of a package), **Rainforest Tours**, **Air Guyana Tours** and **Wonderland Tours**. Other options are Kaieteur Falls with **Baganara Island Resort** for US$245 pp or with **Arrowpoint** for US$275 pp. To charter a plane privately costs US$1200 to Kaieteur and Orinduik. Scheduled flights are the cheapest but are difficult to organize because you have to ask the airlines in person and the itinerary outward and return depends on what other stops are being made en route. **Air Services Ltd** is most frequent with a shuttle to **Mahdia**, from where flights go to other outlying destinations, eg Kaieteur every 3-4 days; you may have to wait a couple of hours in Mahdia while other destinations are served. A tour without transfers or food, but a local guide, costs US$130-145 pp; flight must be full, last-minute cancellations are not uncommon. Tour operators such as **Dagron Tours** (page 49), **Rainforest Tours** (page 50) and **Wilderness Explorers** (page 50) in Georgetown offer overland trips to Kaieteur. Contact them for details of the route and what is included. Minibuses run daily from Georgetown as far as Mahdia, via Mabura Hill.

Iwokrama
Road
1¼ hrs by road from **Annai** or **Surama**. Coming from **Georgetown**, you have to cross the Essequibo at Kurupukari;

ferry runs 0600-1700, hoot for service, US$35 for a car, pick-up or small minibus, US$55 for 15-seat minibus, US$125 truck. The entrances open to coincide with the Georgetown–Lethem buses. At each a passenger manifest is checked to ensure that no one has left the bus in the reserve to hunt. The northern entrance also has a customs point.

On the Rupununi
In 2016 local airlines only provided flights between Georgetown and Lethem, with no intermediate stops. In 2017 **Air Services Ltd** reintroduced a twice-weekly flight to Annai, but on a trial basis only. Transport around the Rupununi is difficult; there are a few 4WD vehicles and some lodges have their own converted Bedford trucks, but moped, bicycle and horse are more common on the rough roads. You can take the Lethem–Georgetown minibuses and get off at Annai, about US$20, 3 hrs from Lethem, or the **Surama** junction (see above).

Annai
Road
The **Rock View Lodge** is an ideal hub for the North Rupununi as it is beside the Annai airstrip, 2 km off the Georgetown–Lethem road, and close to the Rupununi river, offering air, road and river transportation. Rock View–Georgetown by minibus (see under Lethem), or Land Rover US$50-60 return. From Karanambu to Rock View by boat and jeep costs US$380 for up to 4 people, fascinating trip.

Lethem
At the **Rupununi Eco Hotel** (see page 45), ask for Daniel, the owner, who rents 4WDs and minibuses for

charters in the area; phone numbers and email as above.

Air

TGA flies **Georgetown**–Lethem–Georgetown daily at 0800, return 1000, plus Mon, Fri, Sat 1300, return 1500, 1 hr, US$142 one way, US$268 return. It does not make stops on the way. **ASL** have a scheduled service to Lethem daily at 0930, 1½ hrs. **Air Guyana/Wings** flies Georgetown–Lethem–Georgetown Tue, Thu and Sat. Taxis await flight arrivals at Lethem airport.

Road

The road from **Georgetown** to Lethem, 585 km, via Mabura Hill and Kurupukari is now all-weather, but only the 1st 105 km out of Georgetown are paved. It provides a through route from Georgetown to **Boa Vista** (Brazil). After Linden, it runs 100 km to **Mabura Hill**, then 50 km to **Frenchman's Creek** and on to the Essequibo. After the river and Iwokrama the road goes through jungle to the **Surama** road junction, then on to **Wowetta**, the 1st village in the Savannah. Then the road crosses the **Rupununi**. Minibuses leave when full for Lethem at 1800 (check in at 1700), US$50-60 one way; most can be found on Church St between Cummings St and Light St. Reliable service is provided by **P and A**, and by **Carlie's** (Robb St and Oronoque St,

T699 1339, or 616 5984 (Carly), 617 1339 (Cindy). Most are Mon-Sat, but **Guy Braz**, 28 Sheriff St, Campbellville, T231 9752/3, guybraz_cindy@yahoo.com, operate every day. They take the 0600 ferry over the Essequibo and reach Lethem in the early afternoon. They leave Lethem from their own depots at 1800, stop at **Madonna's** (see page 43) at 2100, then depart at 0330 to catch the first ferry at **Kurupukari**.

Border with Brazil

The simplest way to cross the border from Lethem is to take a taxi from the town or airport to Guyanese immigration. The vehicle waits while you get your stamp and then takes you across the bridge to Policía Federal, US$10 for the journey. Guyanese cars are not allowed to go further into Brazil. Taxi drivers may help with changing money from Guyanese dollars to reais (rates for US dollars are poor). If there is no bus waiting at Policía Federal going to **Boa Vista**, there are cars going to **Bonfim Rodoviária**, on Av São Sebastião about 4 blocks off the main border to Boa Vista highway and 3.5 km from the bridge, or to the **CoopBom** (T095-3552 1357/3623 0644) shared taxi company, 1 long block further into town past Hotel Tacutu at the junction of Av Tuxauá de Farias, opposite Assambléia de Deus, US$3. Shared taxi Bonfim–Boa Vista US$8.75, 1½ hrs.

Suriname

The main attractions of Suriname are the tropical, Amazonian flora and fauna, historic Paramaribo and the ethnic diversity in this sparsely populated country. Much of the interior is untouched and largely uninhabited. Infrastructure is limited, so most tourist lodges, Amerindian and Maroon villages can only be reached by small boat or plane.

Paramaribo
historic buildings and a colourful market

The capital and main port, lies on the Suriname river, 12 km from the sea. There are many beautiful colonial buildings in Dutch (neo-Normanic) style on the waterfront and central streets whose fusion of European architecture and South American craft led to the historic centre's UNESCO listing. Much of the historic centre, dating from the 19th century, and the religious buildings have been restored. The city has an intriguing mixture of cultures and an energetic nightlife.

Fort Zeelandia
Fort Zeelandia houses the **Suriname Museum** ⓘ *T425871, www.surinaams museum.net, Tue-Fri 0900-1400, Sun 1000-1400, US$2.75, free guided tours Sun 1030, 1200, has a café and shop*. All the historic buildings in the complex are open to the public. The fort itself now belongs to the **Stichting (foundation) Surinaams Museum** and is part of the **Guiana Shield exchange programme** ⓘ *http:// amazonian-museum-network.org*. It is full of interesting items, archaeological and cultural, up to the present day. Most of the text is in Dutch, a little in English. Don't miss the three Gerrit Schouten (1779-1839) dioramas. There are good views of the river from the ramparts. The wooden officers' houses in the same complex have been restored as well. The 19th-century Roman Catholic **St Peter and Paul Basilica** (1885), built entirely of wood, is one of the largest wooden buildings in the Americas. This twin towered, pale yellow and blue neo-Gothic building with rose windows is both impressive and beautiful. The interior is a delightful play of light on different tones of bare timber. You are asked to dress modestly, cover up arms and legs, and give a donation

> **Tip...**
> Head for Mr F H R Lim A Postraat if you wish to see what Paramaribo looked like only a comparatively short time ago.

Essential Suriname

Finding your feet

The airport is 47 km south of Paramaribo. Most buses congregate in a chaotic area near the Central Market.

Fact file
Location 5.8333° N, 55.1667° W
Capital Paramaribo
Time zone GMT -4 hrs
Telephone country code +597
Currency Suriname dollar (SRD)

Getting around

There are a few regular bus services from Paramaribo. Private taxis can be expensive; shared taxis are a common way to get around. Car hire is available. Beyond the road network, river boats are the only means of transport, except where charter flights serve communities.

Tip...
In Paramaribo there are many ATMs and cambios for changing euros and dollars into Suriname dollars.

Safety

Paramaribo tends to be safer than Georgetown or Cayenne, but it's still wise to be cautious after dark and take care around the markets and docks. Although beggars and/or drug addicts are a nuisance day or night, they are rarely dangerous.

Do not photograph military installations. If in doubt, ask first.

Fact...
National dress is normally only worn by the Asians on national holidays and at wedding parties, but some Javanese women still go about in sarong and klambi.

Weather Paramaribo

January	February	March	April	May	June
30°C	30°C	31°C	31°C	31°C	31°C
23°C	22°C	22°C	23°C	24°C	23°C
198mm	126mm	111mm	186mm	286mm	316mm

July	August	September	October	November	December
31°C	32°C	32°C	33°C	32°C	31°C
23°C	23°C	23°C	23°C	23°C	23°C
226mm	186mm	100mm	106mm	112mm	192mm

of US$1.35. One of the Caribbean's largest **mosques** is on Keizerstraat (take a magnificent photo at sunset; make an appointment to visit). Next to it is one of the city's two synagogues: **Neve Shalom** (1835-1837), at Keizerstraat 88 (appointment needed to visit), and **Zedek v' Shalom** (1735) on the corner of Klipstenstraat and Heerenstraat. The latter is no longer used as a synagogue, but houses businesses; see www.surinamejewishcommunity.com/synagogues. Also worth seeing are the **Hindu temples** of **Arya Dewakar** on Wanicastraat and **Shri Vishnu Mandir** on Koningstraat. The **Numismatisch Museum** ⓘ *Mr FHR Lim A Postraat 7, T520016, www.cbvs.sr/museum/numis-intro.htm, Mon-Fri 0800-1400*, displaying the history of Suriname's money, is operated by the Central Bank.

On Onafhankelijkheidsplein (Independence Square, originally called Oranjeplein), near Fort Zeelandia, stand the **Presidential Palace** (formerly the Governor's Mansion) and the **Ministry of Finance**, with an octagonal tower. A collection of flags across from the Zeelandia complex is supposed to represent the countries with embassies in Paramaribo. On Sunday mornings you can see birdsong competitions here, a popular custom throughout Suriname. Men carrying their songbird (usually a small black *twa-twa*) in a cage are frequently seen; they may be on their way to and from work or just taking their pet for a stroll. Behind the Presidential Palace is the palm-tree-filled **Palmentuin** ⓘ *0700-2200*, with a bandstand. **Mr FHR Lim A Postraat**, with some of the finest colonial buildings in the city, leads from Onafhankelijkheidsplein to Kerkplein, in the middle of which is the small **Dutch Reformed Church**. A third park is the **Cultuurtuin**, some distance from the centre, which contains the **zoo** ⓘ *open 0900-1800.*

From Fort Zeelandia you can walk past the fine buildings on Water Kant to an area by the waterfront with handicraft stalls and the food stands known as *warungs* (see page 70). Beyond is De Waag restaurant at the foot of Keizerstraat and the area where buses congregate and pirogues wait to ferry people over the river to Meerzorg. Further still is the **Central Market** ⓘ *Mon-Fri 0700-1700, Sat till 1400*, with fruit, vegetables, fish, etc, downstairs, clothes and hardware upstairs. Almost next to it is the **Vreedzaam Market** (witches' or Maroon market) for medicinal herbs, remedies and potions. It's best to go with a local to explain things. There is a **Javanese market** area on Jozef Israelstraat in northern Paramaribo and a **Chinese market** on Tourtonnelaan, both on Sunday morning.

Leonsberg and Nieuw-Amsterdam

An interesting excursion for a half or full day is to take a city bus, or taxi, past Stinasu and the Courtyard Marriott to **Leonsberg**, a northeastern suburb of Paramaribo on the Suriname river (restaurants overlook the water). Here you can take a dolphin tour (see What to do, page 73) or other river tours.

Alternatively, a ferry crosses the river to Nieuw-Amsterdam, the capital of the predominantly Javanese district of **Commewijne** at the confluence of Suriname and Commewijne rivers. There's an open-air **museum** ⓘ *open Mon-Fri 0900-1700, weekends 1000-1800, US$0.85, over 60s and under 9s half price*, inside the old fortress that guarded the rivers' confluence. There are nice gardens with old buildings, some military items, displays on slave history, a café and exhibitions in the old prison. The Leonsberg ferry goes to within walking distance of the fort. From Nieuw-Amsterdam you can return to Paramaribo over the spectacular, steeply raked **Jules Wijdenbosch bridge** at Meerzorg, which has wonderful views eastwards by day and over the city lights at night. You can walk over the bridge, but not ride a bicycle (you can walk it across). On 1 January there is a 5-km walk over the bridge. Below is the city's main port for commercial shipping. To get to Nieuw-Amsterdam by bus, take any bus from Paramaribo over the Meerzorg bridge, US$0.15, ask to be let out at the junction of Commissaris Thurkowweg and then catch a bus towards Mariënburg, US$0.20. Again, ask where to get off and walk 1 km to the fort. There are also ferries from Paramaribo, near the bus station, to Meerzorg. A taxi between Paramaribo and Nieuw-Amsterdam costs US$10.

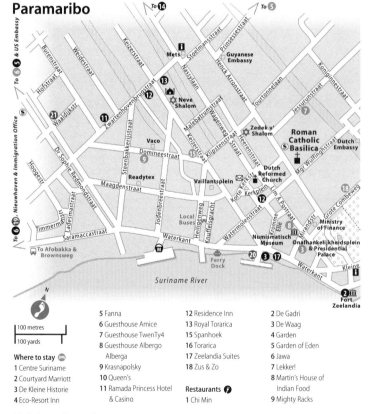

Paramaribo

Where to stay
1 Centre Suriname
2 Courtyard Marriott
3 De Kleine Historie
4 Eco-Resort Inn
5 Fanna
6 Guesthouse Amice
7 Guesthouse TwenTy4
8 Guesthouse Albergo Alberga
9 Krasnapolsky
10 Queen's
11 Ramada Princess Hotel & Casino
12 Residence Inn
13 Royal Torarica
15 Spanhoek
16 Torarica
17 Zeelandia Suites
18 Zus & Zo

Restaurants
1 Chi Min
2 De Gadri
3 De Waag
4 Garden
5 Garden of Eden
6 Jawa
7 Lekker!
8 Martin's House of Indian Food
9 Mighty Racks

West of Paramaribo

A narrow but paved road leads through the citrus- and vegetable-growing areas of **Wanica** and **Saramacca**, linked by a bridge over the Saramacca river. At Boskamp (90 km from Paramaribo) is the **Coppename river**. The Coppename bridge crosses to **Jenny** on the west bank. The Coppename Estuary is the 12,000-ha Coppenamemonding Nature Reserve, a RAMSAR site protecting many shorebird colonies, mangrove and other (see www.ramsar.org and www.whsrn.org).

A further 50 km is **Totness**, where there was an early 19th-century Scottish settlement, one of several sugar- and cotton-growing plantations in the area known as **Seacoast**. It is the largest village in the Coronie district, along the coast between Paramaribo and Nieuw-Nickerie on the Guyanese border. There is a good government guesthouse. The road (liable to flooding) leads through an extensive forest of coconut palms. **Wageningen**, 40 km further west and 5 km south of the main road, is a modern little town, the centre of the Suriname rice-growing area. One of the largest fully mechanized rice farms in the world was established here. The **Bigi-Pan** area (68,320 ha, see www.whsrn.org) comprises lagoons, mangroves and mudflats and is a birdwatchers' paradise (scarlet ibis, flamingos, herons, waders, birds of prey, also caiman). Boats may be hired from local fishermen. METS includes Bigi Pan in its two-day tours to **Nickerie**, US$252, other agencies US$105-160 for two days, US$165-190 for three days. Visitors stay at a lodge, Stephanie's, on the lagoon.

Nieuw-Nickerie on the south bank of the Nickerie river 5 km from its mouth, opposite Guyana, is the main town and port of the Nickerie district, distinguished for its rice fields. It's a clean, ordered town with a sizeable East Indian population and a lot of mosquitoes.

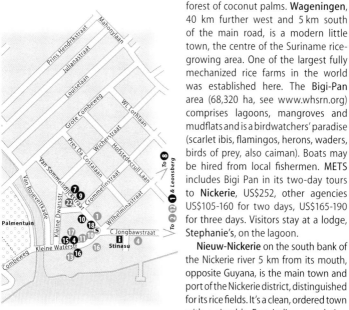

10 Pannekoek en Poffertjes Café
11 Power Smoothie
12 Roopram Rotishop
13 Roti Joosje
14 Spice Quest
15 't Vat
16 Tangelo
17 Warungs
18 Zanzibar

Bars & clubs
19 Ballroom Energy
20 Broki
21 Touché
22 Zuid

Border with Guyana

Ferry to Moleson Creek (for Springlands) From South Drain/Canawaima (Suriname, 40 km from Nieuw-Nickerie, excellent road) to

Moleson/Crabwood Creek (Guyana), it's a 30-minute trip on the ferry. Immigration forms are handed out on the boat. Queues can be long and slow to enter Suriname. Suriname is one hour ahead of Guyana. If entering Suriname from Guyana, you can change money at a hut at the ferry point or, failing that, at one of several banks in Nieuw-Nickerie. On departure, you can change Suriname dollars into Guyanese or US dollars at Corriverton or in Georgetown. The Guyanese embassy in Paramaribo is at Henck Arronstraat 82, T477895, guyembassy@sr.net (dress smartly – no shorts, flip flops, vests, leggings or sleaveless shirts), and the consulate in Nieuw-Nickerie is at Gouveneur Straat and West Kanaal Straat 10, T211019, guyconsulnick@sr.net. In 2017 finance was being sought for a bridge across the Corentyne.

Blanche Marie Falls, 320 km from Paramaribo on the road to Apoera on the Corantijn river, is a popular destination. **Washabo** near Apoera, which has an airstrip, is an Amerindian village. No public transport runs from Paramaribo to the Apoera-Bakhuis area, but operators run tours to Blanche Marie and Apoera, from US$345-370 per person for four days, US$475 for five days, minimum five people (www.blanche-marie.com) and there are charter flights to the Washabo airstrip. Irregular small boats sail from Apoera to Nieuw-Nickerie and to Springlands (Guyana).

East of Paramaribo to Guyane

Leaving the traffic jams of Paramaribo behind, the main highway crosses the Meerzorg bridge (see page 60) and runs through eastern Suriname to Albina on the border with Guyane, passing through the districts of Commewijne and Marowijne. There are some interesting plantation estates left in the Commewijne district. A popular site *near the junction of main road to Albina and the road to Nieuw-Amsterdam* is the **Peperpot Nature Park** ① *T354547, Facebook: peperpotnaturepark, open daily 0800-1700, US$3.20*, a former cacao and coffee estate with nature trails and a historic plantation village. Tours from Paramaribo cost US$41-77, by bus or bicycle; buses from Meerzorg daily 0600-0900 and 1300-1800, none on Sunday, US$0.15, 10 minutes.

Frederiksdorp ① *www.frederiksdorp.com*. Dating from around 1760, **Frederiksdorp** is a beautiful plantation close to the Commewijne river. It can be reached by ferry from Mariënburg (US$4 for the boat); journey time from Paramaribo one hour. The old buildings – **Plantation House**, **Doctor's House** and the **police houses** – are a World Heritage Site and have been converted into hotel accommodation for families. Brand new bungalows have been built, with local furnishings, for couples. The restaurant serves local food with a European touch. There is a swimming pool with a wooden deck. Staff come from surrounding Javanese and Hindustani villages. About 10 minutes' walk away is the Hindustani and Moslem village of **Johanna en Margaretha**, with bars and eating places. From here

Fact...
More old plantation houses are included on tours called the Sugar Trail, eg Concordia and Mariënburg, together with villages, ruined mills and the town of Tamanredjo (see below). Tour price about US$68, including boat rides from Paramaribo.

boat trips go into the 'swamps', or former paddy fields, which is a great area for birdwatching. To reach this area boats have to be hauled across the dam which separates the freshwater canals from the brackish swamps. Beyond the swamps boats can go all the way to the beach at Matapica (see below), where turtles can be seen nesting (mosquitoes can be a problem at dusk). A three-day/two-night package costs US$370, including all transfers, meals, excursions and activities (except turtle watching). They also have a boat, Mi Gudu, with six cabins for transport to Paramaribo, with dinners, parties, yoga trips, moonlight and longer voyages. If you don't want to stay at Frederiksdorp, there are day cycle tours costing about US$60.

Wia-Wia Nature Reserve The northeast coast of Suriname is known as a major nesting site for sea turtles (five species including the huge leatherback turtle come ashore to lay their eggs). But Commewijne district also has all the mammals and birds you would find inland, plus coastal birds and mangroves. Wia-Wia Nature Reserve protects 36,000 ha and is especially rich in nesting grounds for local and migratory birds (see www.whsrn.org). Sea turtles used to nest here, but the beaches and turtles have shifted westwards out of the reserve to the Matapica area. Turtles can be observed from February to mid-August, but different species arrive at different times (April to June are the best months to visit as you can see adults coming ashore to lay eggs and hatchlings rushing to the sea at high tide). **Jenny Tours** ① *Waterkant 5c (in Broki), Paramaribo, T885 8495, http://suriname-tour.com,* offers two-day tours which go to **Mariënburg**, then a boat to Johanna en Margaretha (see above), where you change to another boat for the one-hour ride through the swamps to **Matapica**. Trips costs US$100 per person, minimum two people. Suitable waterproof clothing should be worn.

The main road goes through **Tamanredjo**, with many new houses and oriental supermarkets, to the bridge over the Commewijne near Sigaripabo. Just beyond is a police checkpoint at Stolkertsijver. Just before Moengo (160 km up the Cottica river from Paramaribo), there is one very short, rough stretch where you should not linger. Apart from this, the road is in good condition, continuing through forest to **Albina** on the Marowijne river. Along the way there are small communities with new buildings, recovering from the destruction of the 1980s civil war. Albina is quite a small town with shops, a market and restaurants.

Galibi Nature Reserve ① *US$2.75 entrance fee, local guide US$10/day.* From Albina it is a two-hour boat trip (including 30 minutes on the open sea) to **Galibi**. Here you can stay at **Stinasu's Warana Lodge**, which has cooking facilities, a refrigerator, rooms with shower and toilet, powered mostly by solar energy. Make arrangements through Stinasu or operators who run all-inclusive, two- and three-day tours from February to September, US$160-200 per person, minimum three (see Stinasu, page 73, www.galibi-suriname.com or tour operators' websites); **METS charges** US$245 for two days, US$294 for three days; **Myrysji Tours** ① *Crommelinstraat 31, Paramaribo, T422550, www.galibi-tours.com,* have tours staying at their own lodge at **Christiaankondre** at the mouth of the Marowijne river. Some tours include St-Laurent du Maroni.

Border with Guyane Customs and immigration on both sides close at 1900, but in Albina staff may leave by 1700. Boats across the river to St-Laurent du Maroni, Guyane, leave from two places: the Bac car ferry is the official crossing; unofficial pirogues leave from another dock close by (see Transport, page 75). Whatever craft you take to enter Suriname, you must get your passport stamped at immigration at the Bac terminal. **Note** You must obtain a tourist card in advance from the consulate in Cayenne or St-Laurent; if you need a visa, check regulations before arrival. Likewise in St-Laurent, where there are two different docks, immigration is at the Bac terminal. There is an official *cambio* in Albina, **Imex**, outside the Bac/immigration terminal, which changes dollars, euros and Suriname dollars (opens at 0800). Since there is no legal money exchange in St-Laurent, if you have no euros get them here when crossing to Guyane as you will need them for the ferry, buses and taxis. Suriname dollars are not recognized in Guyane. If taking a car into Suriname, remember that vehicles drive on the left.

South of Paramaribo

About 5 km from the **International Airport** there is a resort called **Colakreek** ① *Facebook: colakreek, US$2.75 day visit for adults, reductions for children, pay extra for picnic sites, cabins, etc*, so named for the colour of the water, but good for swimming (busy at weekends), lifeguards, water bicycles, children's village, restaurant, bar, tents or huts for overnight stay. It is managed by **METS** and there are plenty of package tours and combinations available from US$91 in cabin for four for overnight accommodation, day tours from US$95; www.mets.sr. The village of **Bersaba**, 40 km from Paramaribo close to the road to the airport, is a popular area for the **Coropinakreek**. Many people go there at weekends and holidays, as well as to the neighbouring village of **Republiek**. Tour operators sell kayaking trips at Coropina for about US$75 for one day.

Santigron About 30 km southwest of Paramaribo, via **Lelydorp** (District Wanica; Hotel De Lely, Sastrodisomoweg 41; The Lely Hills hotel and casino, T366289, http://lelyhills.creativewebsuriname.com), is the Maroon village of **Santigron**, on the east bank of the Saramacca river, founded in 1900 by the Saramaccans. Today other Maroons also live here, with 500 people in the village. A community tourism project, **Santigron Experience** ① *T874 6610, www.santigron.com*, organizes one-day tours, with a boat trip on the Saramacca river, or a cultural dance performance, US$60-85 (prices vary according to number of people, website has details and departure dates; other agencies sell tours). They also offer two-day tours for US$170. You can also stay in B&B accommodation with dinner for US$48 per person. Minibuses leave Paramaribo for Santigron at 0530 and 1500, two hours, US$0.40. They return as soon as they have dropped off passengers in the village, so make sure you will have a bus to return on. Nearby is the Amerindian village of **Pikin Poika**. These two villages make a good independent day trip.

Jodensavanne and around You can drive to **Jodensavanne** (Jews' Savannah, established 1639), south of Paramaribo on the opposite bank of the Suriname river, where three cemeteries (two Jewish, one for slaves) and the foundations of one of the oldest synagogues in the Western Hemisphere, Bracha v' Shalom, have been restored (www.jodensavanne.sr.org; also www.surinamejewishcommunity.com/synagogues). This was the largest Jewish settlement in the Western Hemisphere at the time. You can also visit the healing well. It is one to 1½ hours with a suitable vehicle; the road can be bad in the rainy season. The route is via the Martin Luther Kingweg to **Powakka**, about 90 minutes south of the capital, an Amerindian village of thatched huts and a small church. In the surrounding forest one can pick mangoes and other exotic fruit. The road goes east to the ferry across the Suriname river at **Carolina**, then to **Redi Doti** near Jodensavanne. Tours to Jodensavanne cost from US$87 by boat up the Suriname river, or US$75-115 by bus or car. Some tours include Powakka (eg tours with **Flair's Joden Savanne Experience** trip, T498407, www.tip-suriname.com), others combine with Colakreek or Overbridge (see Where to stay, page 69) and cost up to US$140. **Blakawatra** is a beautiful creek with recreational facilities, not far from Jodensavanne, also included in some tours (full day about US$100). Cassipora bus from Saramaccastraat in Paramaribo goes by Blakawatra and near the Carolina ferry at 0830 daily except Saturday, two hours one way, return also at 0830.

Brokopondo Reservoir You can continue by bus or car to **Afobakka**, south of Powakka, where there is a large dam on the Suriname river. Behind it is the Brokopondo reservoir, or Professor Doctor Ingenieur W J van Blommestein Meer, built in the 1960s to provide electricity for the bauxite industry. Thousands of hectares of forest were submerged and the skeletons of the trees can still be seen in the water. The **Afobaka Resort** ⓘ http://afobakaresort.com, is on the Suriname river, below the dam. It has lodges for six to 12 people (from US$35 per person midweek), all meals extra, with boat and kayak trips and other activities. Bus Paramaribo (Saramaccastraat, near Tropicana Casino) to Afobakka, three hours, US$1.05, at 0600 and 1300, 0830 on Sunday, and to Brokopondo at 0700 and 1330, none on Sunday, US$1.20, three hours. Near Brokopondo, set in tropical forest on the banks of the Suriname river, is the **Bergendal Eco & Cultural River Resort** ⓘ *Domineestraat 39, Paramaribo, T475050, www.bergendalresort.com; book online, or via the Hotel Krasnopolsky*, 85 km/1½ hours by road and river from the capital. Day visits and overnight stays in three types of comfortable cabins are offered. Activities include canopy zip-line, hiking, mountain bikes, kayaking and nature tours.

Brownsberg National Park ⓘ *US$2.75, guide US$9.75.* An hour by car from Brokopondo, are the hills of Brownsberg National Park which overlook the **Brokopondo lake**. It features good walking to four waterfalls – **Leo**, **Irene**, **Koemboe** and **Mazaroni** – and to the viewpoint at **Mazaroni Top**. Trails vary in length from less than 1 km to 4.5 km and can be walked with or without a guide. There are ample chances to see wildlife (it includes 400 species of bird). **Stinasu** manages the facilities and it, and other tour operators, run all-inclusive tours from Paramaribo (two-day tours from US$150, price includes transport, accommodation, food and guide; one-day tour with an agency costs from

US$65-94). Independent visits are possible, but you must pay the entrance fee, and arrange accommodation in advance at Stinasu's guesthouses, campsite or hammock place (from US$5.50 camping to US$8.50 for a bed). Take your own food. If not in your own car (there is parking fee too, US$1.50), you can take the Afobakka bus, as above, to the village of **Brownsweg** (US$1.05, three hours) and ask for a car to take you to Brownsberg, or walk 7 km. **Tukunari Island**, in the lake, is a two-hour canoe ride from the Afobakka dam. The island is near the village of **Lebi Doti**, where Aucaner Maroons relocated when the reservoir waters rose. Tours go to Tukunari (the local name for peacock bass), to other islands and to the **Ston Island peninsula** (US$95 with boat tour). Several agencies offer fishing tours on the lake.

The road south of Brownsberg ends at **Pokigron** (also called Atjoni). Beyond here progress up the Suriname river is by boat. Several tour operators organize stays in lodges (see page 69).

Saramacca villages and Awarradam There are many **Saramacca villages** along the Gran Rio and Pikin Rio, both Suriname river tributaries. These are fascinating places, set up in the 17th and 18th centuries by escaped slaves, originally from Ghana, who preserve a ceremonial language, spirituality and traditions. METS has a comfortable lodge on the Gran Rio at **Awarradam**, on an island in front of a beautiful set of rapids in thick forest, and many other agencies organize culturally sensitive tours to the villages. Independent visitors are also welcome.

In the far south of Suriname are a series of dramatic granite mountains rising out of pristine forest. The highest is **Mount Kasikasima** (718 m), near the Trio and Wajana Amerindian village of **Palumeu** on the Upper Tapanahony river. METS has a comfortable river lodge here and visitors learn about the lifestyle of the villagers. They and other operators also organize expeditions to the mountain, which involve a two-day boat trip and a strenuous six- to seven-hour climb, rewarded by incredible views over the rainforest. METS tours to Awarradam are four to five days, US$645 per person (from US$570 with other agencies); Awarradam and the Gran Rio river jungle camp, five days US$675; Palumeu, four to five days, US$645 with METS, from US$570 with other agecies; Kasikasima, five days, US$845; Kasikasima, eight days, US$895. Combinations of Awarradam and Palumeu and Awarradam and Kasikasima are available.

Central Suriname Nature Reserve This reserve (1.592 million ha – 9.7% of Suriname's total land area) is now part of the UNESCO's World Heritage list. Raleigh/Voltzberg Reserve has been joined with Tafelberg and Eilerts de Haan reserves to create this enormous area, some of which is yet to be explored. **Raleighvallen/Voltzberg Nature Reserve** ⓘ *US$2.75 for the 1st night, US$1.35 for each following night*, covering 78,170 ha, is a rainforest park, southwest of Paramaribo, on the Coppename river. It includes **Foengoe (Fungu) Island** in the river and **Voltzberg peak**. Climbing the mountain (240 m) at sunrise is an unforgettable experience. The climb up takes four hours and is usually done on the second day of the tour. On the third day visitors are taken to the falls. There is good birdwatching in the reserve and eight species of monkey have been recorded. The reserve can be reached by air or by road (180 km, four hours) followed by a three- to four-hour boat ride. Tourist facilities are on Foengoe Island, to which **Stinasu** do four-day tours, all-inclusive with transport, food and guides from US$320 (www.raleighvallen.com). Lodging is in rooms with and without bath (priced accordingly) or in hammocks (if you don't have your own you can rent one). Other operators go through Stinasu.

Stoelmanseiland and Maroon villages **Stoelmanseiland**, on the Lawa river in the interior near the border with Guyane, and the Maroon villages and rapids in the area can be visited on an organized tour of three, five or eight days, but no company offers this trip as a regular feature. Visitors have to make special arrangements. They are, however, more easily reached by river from St-Laurent du Maroni and Maripasoula in Guyane.

Listings Suriname *map page 60.*

Tourist information

Suriname Tourist Foundation
Main office JF Nassylaan 2, T424878, www.surinametourism.sr. Mon-Fri 0730-1500. Branch offices at the Zeelandia Complex, T479200. Mon-Fri 0800-1330, and Johan Adolf Pengel airport.

Where to stay

Service charge at hotels is 5-10%.

Paramaribo

$$$$-$$$ Courtyard Marriott
Anton Dragtenweg 52-54, T456000, www.marriott.com/pbmcy.
About 1 km from Torarica on the road towards Leonsberg, not possible to walk beside the river, so take a taxi or the hotel's shuttle bus to Krasnapolsky. 5 types of room, all spacious and comfortable, with pool, gym, live music, both restaurants have a dedicated kitchen, themed culinary evenings, **Martini'Bar** cocktail lounge, popular. Works in partnership with **Conservation International**.

$$$$-$$$ Krasnapolsky
Domineestraat 39, T475050, www.krasnapolsky.sr.
A/c, in business district, 4 standards of room, travel agency, shopping centre, good breakfast and buffet, 5 eating options, swimming pool with bar with view over city, business centre and conference facilities, airport shuttle.

$$$$-$$$ Torarica
Mr Rietbergplein 1, T471500, www.torarica.com.
One of the best in town, very pleasant, family-oriented resort, book ahead, swimming pool and other sports facilities, sauna, casino, tropical gardens, pier over the river, a/c, 2 restaurants (**Plantation Room** for lunch and dinner, local and international food; **The Edge**, for drinks and snacks, open 0900-0100), also has **The Lounge** for drinks and snacks, Sun-Thu 1000-2400, Fri-Sat 1000-0130 (see **Tangelo** under Restaurants, page 71); good poolside buffet on Fri evening, superb breakfast, business centre.

$$$ Eco-Resort Inn
Cornelis Jongbawstraat 16, T425522,
www.ecoresortinn.com.
Part of **Torarica** group with use of the
resort facilities, good atmosphere and
value, breakfast included, restaurant
(**$$**), bar, helpful staff, business centre.

$$$ Queen's
Kleine Waterstraat 15, T474969,
www.queenshotelsuriname.com.
Including breakfast, service charge and
tax. A/c, 3 types of room, fitness centre,
minibar, Garden restaurant and bar
below (10% discount for guests) and
Euphoria nightclub.

$$$ Residence Inn
Anton Dragtenweg 7, T521414,
www.residenceinn.sr.
Minibar, laundry, including breakfast, in a
residential area, pool, tennis court, a/c bar
and **Matutu** restaurant, European and
Surinamese food (**$$**), airport transfer.

$$$ Royal Torarica
Kleine Waterstraat 10, T473500,
www.royaltorarica.com.
Sister hotel of **Torarica**. More for
business than leisure, but comfortable
rooms, river view, pool and other sports
facilities, lobby restaurant.

$$$ Spanhoek
Domineestraat 2-4 (entrance
on Keiserstraat), T477888,
www.spanhoekhotel.com.
Boutique hotel in business district,
funky, trendy decor, lovely bathrooms,
continental breakfast with Surinamese
delicacies, restaurant on 1st floor. Always
ask about discounts if visiting in person,
also long-term rentals. Has sidewalk café,
Terras, for drinks and snacks. There is a
cambio in the same building.

$$$-$$ Zeelandia Suites
Kleine Waterstraat 1a, T424631,
www.zeelandiasuites.com.
Smart, business-style suites with
comfy rooms and all mod cons in
same precinct as **'t Vat** (see page 70).

$$ Guesthouse Albergo Alberga
Lim A PoStraat 13, T520050, www.
guesthousealbergoalberga.com.
Central, in a 19th-century house,
pleasant, terrace and TV area, simple,
spotless rooms, a/c or fan (cheaper),
breakfast extra, pool, good value, book in
advance. Steep spiral staircase to 1st floor.

$$ Guesthouse Amice
Gravenberchstraat 5 (10 mins from centre),
T434289, www.guesthouse-amice.sr.
Quiet area, room with balcony more
expensive, a/c, comfortable, breakfast,
airport transfer and tours available.

$$ Hotel Centre Suriname
Van Sommelsdijck-straat 4, T426310,
www.hotelcentresuriname.com.
A/c, good value, convenient, several
places to eat nearby, parking.

$$ Zus & Zo
Grote Combeweg 13a, T520905, www.
twenty4suriname.com/zusenzo.html.
In a large green colonial building opposite
Palmentuin (see page 59), small but
functional rooms, shared bath, cheaper
with fan, use of washing machine, no
kitchen but has a popular café open daily
0800-2300, arts and crafts centre, special
events most nights: food, drink, films or
music. In same group as **Guesthouse
TwenTy4** and **Fiets** cycle agency.

$$-$ De Kleine Historie
Dr JC De Mirandastraat 8, T521007,
www.dekleinehistorieguesthouse.com.
Guesthouse with rooms for up to 6
with a/c and one dorm for 6 in bunks

with fan (US$12 per bed), shared bath, breakfast included. Balconies, sitting room, cooking lessons (but no kitchen), very convenient for historic centre, clean, simple, very welcoming and helpful.

$$-$ Guesthouse TwenTy4
Jessurunstraat 24, T420751, http://twenty4suriname.com.
Big pale blue-and-white house, simple but well-maintained rooms, cheaper with shared bath and fan, bar, buffet breakfast extra, Wi-Fi, pleasant, "backpackers' paradise".

$ Fanna
Prinsessestraat 31, T476789, www. appartementsuriname.com.
From a/c with bath to basic, breakfast extra, safe, family-run, pool, kitchen, washing machine, English spoken.

West of Paramaribo

$$$ Residence Inn
R P Bharosstraat 84, Nieuw Nickerie, T210950, www.residenceinn.sr.
Best in town, prices higher at weekend, central, a/c, bath, hot water, laundry, good restaurant (**Matutu**, **$$**), bar.

$ Ameerali
Maynardstraat 32-36, Nieuw Nickerie, T231212.
A/c, good, restaurant (**$$**) and bar.

South of Paramaribo

$$$$ De Plantage
Km 23.5 on the east–west road at Tamanredjo, Commewijne, 40 mins from Paramaribo, T356567, www. deplantagecomme wijne.com.
Price is for 2-night stay. Lovely chalets for 2-4 on an old cocoa plantation, restaurant, pool, jungle walks and

observation tower, bicycles for rent. Transfer from Paramaribo US$21.50.

$$$ Overbridge River Resort
1 hr south of the capital, via Paranam (30 km), then 9.5 km to Powerline mast 20-21, then 7.5 km to resort, or 60 km by boat down Suriname river. Reservations, Oude Charlesburgweg 47, Paramaribo, T422565, www.overbridge.net.
Cabins by the river and a white-sand beach, price includes breakfast, weekend and other packages available and tours to nearby sights such as Jodensavanne and Brownsberg.

Lodges on the Upper Suriname river

$$$ Danpaati River Lodge
Prinsessestraat 37, T471113, www.danpaati. net (in the same group as Access Suriname Travel and Frederiksdorp – see page 62).
On an island, 345 km south of Paramaribo, Danpaati offers 3- and 4-day packages, from US$356-420 in bungalows ranging from luxury to family and double cabins. Closely associated with the village of Dan, where visitors can get involved in workshops, etc. It has an associated health care project, genuine community experience, very friendly, excursions to the forest and on the river, yoga classes, swimming pool.

$$$ Anaula Nature Resort
Wagenwegstraat 55, Paramaribo, T410700, www.anaulanatureresort.com.
A comfortable resort near the Ferulassi Falls about 1 hr's boat trip from Pokigron village, 4 hrs' drive from Paramaribo (or reached by air). It has lodges for 2-5 people, cold water, restaurant and bar, swimming pool; activities include forest and Maroon village excursions; 3- and 4-day packages from US$255-300 pp, all inclusive.

Restaurants

Paramaribo

There are some good restaurants, mainly Indonesian and Chinese. Most international-style places and several bars are in the Kleine Waterstraat/Van Sommelsdijkstraat area, opposite the Torarica.

Blauwgrond, north of the city, near Leonsberg, is the area for typical, cheap, largely Indonesian food, served in *warungs* (Indonesian for restaurants). Try a *rijsttafel* in a restaurant such as **Sarinah** (open-air dining), Verlengde Gemenelandsweg 187, T430661, see Facebook. Foodstalls on Waterkant serve mostly Javanese food on polystyrene plates with plastic cutlery; cheap and cheerful. Try *bami* (spicy noodles) and *petjil* (vegetables), recommended on Sun when the area is busiest. In restaurants, a dish to try is *gadogado*, an Indonesian vegetable and peanut concoction.

$$$ Spice Quest
Dr Nassylaan 107, T520747, SpiceQuest on Facebook. Open 1100-1500, 1800-2300, closed Mon.
Creative menu, open-air and indoor seating, Japanese-style setting. Recommended.

$$$-$$ De Waag
Waterkant 5, T474514, www.dewaag.sr. Breakfast, lunch and dinner.
Upmarket bodega and grill in a historic building where slaves were weighed and sold, indoor and outdoor eating, daily and weekly specials, tapas and wines.

$$ Chi Min
Cornelis Jongbawstraat 83, T412324, http://chimin-restaurant.com.
For well-prepared Chinese food, best to book ahead. Recommended.

Tip...
Meat and noodles from stalls in the market are very cheap.

$$ Garden
Opposite Torarica, next to 't Vat, T474979, Facebook: TheGardensu. Open 1700-0100.
Local and international cuisine, part of **Queen's Hotel**, shows in **Euphoria** nightclub (euphoriaparamaribo on Facebook).

$$ Garden of Eden
Virolastraat via Johannes Mungrastraat, T499448.
Attractive garden area and lounge bar/restaurant serving Thai food.

$$ Jawa
Kasabaholoweg 7, T492691.
Famous Indonesian restaurant.

$$ Martin's House of Indian Food
Hajarystraat 19, T473413, www.appartementenbina.com/restaurant/. Open 1100-2300.
Good value and tasty Indian food with friendly service and covered outside dining, plenty of vegetarian options.

$$ 't Vat
Kleine Waterstraat 1, Facebook: 't Vat Sidewalk Café. Daily early till late.
Sidewalk café and sports bar with light meals, snacks and drinks, very popular after work for early evening meeting and drinking. The place to be for the New Year street parties.

$$ Zanzibar
Van Sommelsdijkstraat 1, next to Multi Track Cambio, T471848. Tue-Sun 2000 till late.
Surinamese and international cuisine, entertainment.

$$-$ Lekker!
Van Sommelsdijckstraat22, T472722,
www.lekkerparamaribo.com.
Open 0800-1600.
For upmarket sandwiches, salads, soup,
pasta, desserts and drinks, popular for
business lunch, good service.

$$-$ Roopram Rotishop
Zwartenhovenbrugstraat 23,
T478816, and Watermolenstraat 37.
Mon-Sat 0800-1500.
Rotis and accompanied fillings in fast-food
style dining rooms, generous portions.
Has several other outlets in the city.

$$-$ Tangelo
Kleine Waterstraat, between Torarica
and Royal Torarica, part of same group.
Open 0800-0100.
Coffee shop with snacks, cakes and
desserts, has outside terrace, good.

$ De Gadri
Zeelandiaweg 1, T420688.
Open 0800-2200.
Good location, view of river and close to
Fort Zeelandia. Surinamese main dishes
and snacks and sandwiches.

$ Pannekoek en Poffertjes Café
Van Sommelsdijckstraat 11, T422914.
Thu, Sun 1000-2300, Fri-Sat 1000-0100.
Specializes in 200 different sorts of
pancakes; other dishes too. Under
same ownership is **Mighty Racks**,
Sommelsdijckstraat 16, T520458, with
a dinosaur at the front, specializing in
beef ribs.

$ Power Smoothie
Zwartenhovenbrugstraat 62 (Mon-Fri
0800-2100, Sat 0800-1500) and in
Hermitage Mall, Lalla Rookhweg
(Mon-Sat 0900-2100, Sun 1600-2100),
www.powersmoothiesuriname.com.

Healthy fast food and juice bars in centre
and Hermitage Mall, east of centre.

$ Roti Joosje
Zwartenhovenbrugstraat 9,
T472606, Facebook: rotishopjoosje.
Open 0800-2200.
Well-known, well-liked roti shop in
centre of town, a/c, long-established.
Has other branches.

Bars and clubs

Paramaribo
For nightly activity, go to the Kleine
Waterstraat/Van Sommelsdijckstraat
area. There are also many casinos in the
city, including the **Ramada Princess
Hotel and Casino** opposite the Torarica
and at major hotels.

Ballroom Energy
L'Hermitageweg 25, T497534.
Younger crowd.

Broki
Waterkant 5C, next to the Ferry Docks,
T880 5472, Facebook: BrokiCafe.
Hammock bar, terrace overlooking river,
good food and atmosphere.

Rumors Grand Café
In the lobby of Hotel Krasnapolsky,
T475050. Open 0900-2200 (from 1400
on Sun).
Every Fri live entertainment (jamming)
with Time Out.

Touché
Waaldijk/Dr Sophie Redmondstraat 60,
T401181, Facebook: clubtouche. Fri-Sat
only 2300.
Small restaurant, the best disco.

> **Tip...**
> The liveliest nights are Thursday
> through to Saturday.

Zuid
Van Sommelsdijckstraat 17, T422928,
see Facebook.
Bar with a good reputation, also has a
grill serving burgers, pizzas.

Shopping

Paramaribo
Arts and crafts
Readytex, *Maagdenstraat 44-48,*
behind Hotel Krasnapolsky, www.
readytexartgallery.com, Mon-Fri 0800-
1630, Sat 0830-1330. An arts, craft and
souvenir shop on several floors, with its
own art gallery, huge selection of items,
including maps.

Bookshops
The kiosk in **Krasnapolsky Hotel**
sells books.
Vaco, *Domineestraat 26, T472545,*
Facebook: BoekhandelVACO, opposite
Krasnapolsky. A large, well-stocked
bookshop, also sells English books;
try here for maps.

Music
The following sell international and
local music on CD: **Beat Street** (Mr J
Lachmonstraat, Facebook: beatstreetsur).
Disco Amigo (Wagenwegstraat,
opposite Theater Star).

Shopping centres
Hermitage Shopping Mall
(Vieruurbloemstraat and Lalla
Rookhweg), 5 mins in taxi south of
centre. The only place open until 2100,
with chemists, money exchange,
top-quality boutiques, coffee shops
and music stores. **Maretraite Mall** (Jan
Steenstraat, Blauwgrond, north of the
city. There are several others.

Supermarkets
Many, well stocked. **Choi's** (Johannes
Mungrastraat 17), some way west
of centre, has excellent selections of
Dutch and other European goods; also
Rossignol Deli in the same complex.
Another branch at the corner of
Thurkowweg and Tweekinderenweg
99, north of centre. **Tulip** supermarket
(Tourtonnelaan 133-135) sells many
North American and European products.

What to do

Paramaribo
Cycling
Cardy Adventures and Bike Rental,
see Tour operators, below.
Fietsen, *Grote Combeweg 13a, behind*
Zus & Zo and in same group (see page 68),
T520781, www.fietseninsuriname.com.
Good-quality bikes for rent from US$3.75
for a city bike to US$26.50 per day for
top-of-the-range racer; US$53-106
deposit depending on bike. Tours with
knowledgeable guides, good value,
bike repair. Recommended.

Tour operators
Look for boards all over the centre
advertising tours. Prices may vary
according to the season; look for special
offers. Tours often require a minimum of
2 or 3 people, sometimes more. Prices of
some tours are given in the text above.
Others include: city tour by bus from
US$30, by bike US$25; Commewijne
boat tour US$66-90; sunset dolphin-
watching tour US$30-40; cookery
workshops from US$32.
Access Suriname Travel, *Prinsessestraat*
37, T424522, www.surinametravel.com.
Sells all major tours in Suriname, partner
in Frederiksdorp and Danpaati (see
Where to stay, above) and can supply

general travel information on the country, good guides, manager Sirano Zalman is most helpful. Recommended.

Moen's Dolphin Tours, *at Leonsberg dock, T08893063, or through tour operators*. Small boat tours to see brackish water or Guiana dolphin, the profosu (*Sotalia Guianensis*), at the confluence of the Suriname and Commewijne rivers, US$42 per boat; daytime and sunset tours. Boats are operated by Moen (pronounced 'Moon') and his sons. Moen is a recognized expert on the dolphins. Other boats offer the tour, but they all follow Moen if he is on the water as his success rate is second-to-none. Recommended.

Cardy Adventures and Bike Rental, *Cornelis Jongbawstraat 31 (near Eco-Resort Inn), T422518, www.cardyadventures.com*. Bike rental (bike rental@cardyadventures.com) and standard and adventure tours throughout the country, English spoken, very helpful, efficient, excellent food.

Discover Suriname Tours, *Kleine Waterstraat 1a, T421818, www.discoversurinametours.com*. At same address as **Zeelandia Suites**, regular tours, adventure and nature tours, jeep safaris and trips to Guyana and Guyane.

METS Travel and Tours (Movement for Eco-Tourism in Suriname), *Dr JF Nassylaan 2, T477088, www.surinamevacations.com. Mon-Fri 0800-1600*. Runs a variety of tours and is involved with various community projects. Several of their trips to the interior are detailed above. They also offer city and gastronomy tours.

Stinasu (Foundation for Nature Conservation), *Cornelis Jongbawstraat 14, T476597, www.stinasu.sr. Mon-Thu 0700-1500, Fri 0700-1430*. Offers reasonably priced accommodation and provides tour guides in the Brownsberg, Raleigh Falls and Galibi nature reserves. You can choose an all-inclusive tour, or go independently whereby you arrange your own transport and food, but have to book lodging and pay entrance fees at Stinasu. Prices given on page 63.

Suriname Experience, *Chopinstraat 27, Ma Retraite 3, Paramaribo North, T453083, www.surinameexperience.com*. Very knowledgeable agency about Suriname.

Tourbox, *Kleine Waterstraat, by 't Vat, T477120, www.tourboxsuriname.nl*. General tours around the country.

Waldo's Travel Service, *Kerkplein 10, T422540, www.waldostravel.sr*. Mostly tours in the Caribbean and worldwide, some local, plus airport transfer service.

Waterproof Tours, *Venusstraat 26 (by appointment), T454434, www.waterproofsuriname.com*. Tours of the waters in and around Suriname, dolphin and caiman watching, birdwatching, river trips, also land-based tours in the country.

Wilderness Explorers, *see page 50, www.wilderness-explorers.com*. Offer a wide range of tours to Suriname, Guyana and French Guyane. They have a UK office (T020-8417 1585) for advice and a list of UK operators who sell trips to the 3 Guianas.

see page 63.
see page 50,

Transport

Paramaribo
Air
Johan Pengel International Airport, www.japi-airport.com, is 47 km south of Paramaribo. Arrivals and Departures are in separate buildings. Be prepared for long queues at immigration and when getting your tourist card. There are food shops outside Departures. Minibus to town costs US$15-20 pp, eg **De Paarl**, Kankantriestraat 42, T403610, Facebook:

garagedepaarl; **Buscovery/Le Grand Baldew**, who have a booth in the Arrival hall, Tourtonnelaan 59, T474713, www.buscoverytours.com/www. legrandbaldew.com, **Waldo's**, see above, US$7 pp; bus costs US$10.50 with **Ashruf** taxi company, T454451 (it makes many stops), taxi proper costs US$25-28, but negotiate. Many hotels offer transfers to and from the international airport for guests with room reservation. There is a guesthouse near the airport (**$$ Sonja Guesthouse**, T680 6105, Facebook: zanderij.guesthouse, some 5 mins away by car). Internal flights and some flights to **Georgetown** leave from **Zorg en Hoop** airfield in a suburb of Paramaribo (on Doekhieweg Oost).

Bus and taxi
There are few regular buses. The majority of services, short- and long-distance, leave from the **bus station** between Heiligenweg and Knuffelsgracht in the centre of Paramaribo, near the market. There is a sales office/waiting room, T472450, www.nvbnvsuriname.com. The information on the website is much less confusing than the timetable on the waiting room wall. The buses themselves are poorly marked and the whole place is chaotic. More buses wait on Waterkant, near Broki nightclub. Also near here is the dock for **pirogues** across the river to Meerzorg. There are privately run 'wild buses', also known as 'numbered buses' which run on fixed routes around the city; they are minivans and are severely overcrowded. Buses have no luggage space. Try to put bags under your seat or you will have to hold them in your lap.

To Nickerie Mon-Sat 0600, 1300 each way, US$1.75. Shared taxis leave from the Central Market, about US$30-35.

Small bus to **Albina** from the bus station daily at 0700, 0830, 1230, except Sun 0830 only, US$1.20, 4 hrs; return from Albina at same times. A shared taxi costs US$22 per person, while a private taxi will charge US$128, about 2 hrs.

Direct minibuses to **Georgetown** via South Drain (fare does not include ferry crossing), are run by many small companies, US$50-60, pick up and drop off at hotels: **Bobby's**, T498583; **Lambada Bus Service**, Keizerstraat 162, T411 073, and **Bin Laden**, T0-210944/0-8809271. You have to change buses once across the border; you are given a card to hand to the bus driver in the next country. **Buscovery/Le Grand Baldew** (address above), organizes 3- and 4-day trips to **Georgetown** and **Cayenne** respectively, US$635 (they also do tours around Suriname).

Car hire
Avis, Kristalstraat 1, T551158, www. avis.com (also at hotels Torarica and Marriott); **De Paarl** (see above under Air); **Europcar**, Kleine Waterstraat 1 (behind 't Vat), T424631, www. europcar.sr, has a fly-drive programme including Guyana – in combination with Wilderness Explorers, see page 50). **Hertz at Real Car**, Van 't Hogerhuysstraat 23,T400409, www.hertz.com; **SPAC**, Verl Gemenelandsweg 139A, T490882. **Wheelz**, HD Benjaminstraat 20, T442929, 08802361 after 1600 and at weekends, www.wheelzcarrental.com.

Taxi
Taxis generally have no meters, average price US$2.50. The price should be agreed upon beforehand. If you're a hotel guest, let the hotel make arrangements.

Tourtonne's Taxi, Tourtonnelaan 142, T475734/425380, www.tourtonnestaxi. com, is recommended. Reliable and good value, also taxi tours, will collect from airport with advance notice.

West of Paramaribo
Bus
See under Paramaribo, above. The Nieuw Nickerie bus station is next to the market on G G Maynardstraat. **Paramaribo–South Drain** costs US$7.

Border with Guyana
Boat
From Nieuw Nickerie to Moleson Creek: the Canawaima ferry sails once or twice a day from South Drain, near Nieuw Nickerie, to **Moleson/Crabwood Creek** depending on demand, US$10 (US$15 with return within 21 days), cars US$30, pick-ups US$40. T212331, or T085 4008 to check when the ferry is running. Taxi bus from Nickerie market to South Drain at 0730, but can pick you up from your hotel.

Border with Guyane
Boat
The vehicle and passenger ferry to **St-Laurent du Maroni, Bac International** *La Gabrielle* (bac.gabrielle@orange.fr) has 3-4 crossings a day, 6 on Sat, 30 mins. Passengers US$5/€4.50 one way, car US$36.75/€34.20, payable only in euros. Service can change at any time. This is the official crossing. Unofficial pirogues cross from another dock nearby, US$5/€4.50 (or US$10.75/€10 for 1 person). See page 80 for immigration details.

Minibuses and taxis
Transport to/from **Paramaribo** waits at the Bac and pirogue docks in Albina (see Transport, Paramaribo, for fares). There is a police check at Stolkertsijver (see page 63). If you did not get an entry stamp into Suriname, you will be in trouble. Some drivers will check that you have a stamp in your passport.

Guyane

Tourism is slowly being developed in Guyane, as in all the Guianas, with the main draws being 'space tourism' at Kourou, birdwatching and adventure trips into the forests.

Cayenne

parks, mansions and museums

The capital and the chief port of Guyane is on the island of Cayenne at the mouth of the Cayenne river. Founded by French traders in the 16th century, but taking its name from an Amerindian prince, Cayenne remained relatively isolated until after the Second World War when Guyane became part of metropolitan France and Rochambeau airport (now called Félix Éboué) was constructed. It retains some of its 18th-century layout.

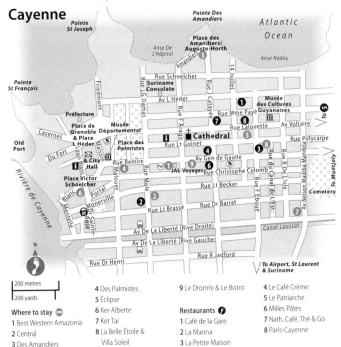

Cayenne

200 metres
200 yards

Where to stay 🛏
1 Best Western Amazonia
2 Central
3 Des Amandiers
4 Des Palmistes
5 Éclipse
6 Ker Alberte
7 Ket Taï
8 La Belle Étoile & Villa Soleil
9 Le Dronmi & Le Bistro

Restaurants 🍴
1 Café de la Gare
2 La Marina
3 La Petite Maison
4 Le Café Crème
5 Le Patriarche
6 Milles Pâtes
7 Nath, Café, Thé & Go
8 Paris-Cayenne

Essential Guyane

Getting around

Domestic flights are heavily booked up, so make your reservations early. The roads are much improved, and *combos*

Fact file
Location 4.0000° N, 53.0000° W
Capital Cayenne
Time zone GMT -3 hrs
Telephone country code +594
Currency Euro (EUR)

Tip...
Most banks have ATMs for cash withdrawals on Visa, sometimes MasterCard. It is almost impossible to change dollars outside Cayenne or Kourou.

(minivans) ply the coastal roads. See also the box, Driving in the Guianas, in Getting around, page 104.

Weather Cayenne

January	February	March	April	May	June
28°C 22°C 456mm	28°C 22°C 305mm	29°C 23°C 402mm	29°C 23°C 405mm	29°C 23°C 592mm	29°C 22°C 462mm

July	August	September	October	November	December
31°C 22°C 238mm	31°C 20°C 172mm	31°C 20°C 98mm	31°C 20°C 103mm	30°C 22°C 163mm	29°C 22°C 360mm

Sights

There are three main parks: the **Place des Palmistes** is a large open space with a variety of palms. Adjoining it is the open **Place de Grenoble** and **Place L Héder**, on which stands the Jesuit-built residence (circa 1890) of the Prefect (La Préfecture), as well as other official buildings. The **Place des Amandiers** (also known as the Place Auguste-Horth) is by the sea; it is a nice place to go at dusk when birds are roosting in the trees and feeding at the water's edge, men play boules and dominoes and people fish and stroll in the fading light. An interesting museum, the **Musée Départemental Alexandre-Franconie** ① *1 ave Général de Gaulle, near the Place de Palmistes, T295913, http://musee.cg973.fr/ws/collections/app/report/index.html, different hours every day, closed Tue, Sun, Thu afternoon and Sat afternoon, US$3.35,* exhibits among other things pickled snakes and the trunk of the 'late beloved twin-trunked palm' of the Place de Palmistes. There is a good entomological collection and excellent paintings of convict life. Next door is the municipal library. The **Musée des Cultures Guyanaises** ① *54 rue Mme Payé, T314172, mcg87@wanadoo.fr, Mon, Tue, Thu 0800-1300, 1500-1745, Wed, Fri 0800-1300, US$2.50, 18-25 year-olds US$1, children free,* has a small collection of crafts from tribal communities. The **market** on Wednesday, Friday and Saturday mornings has a great Caribbean flavour, but is expensive. The **Canal Laussat** (built by Malouet in 1777) marks the boundary of the central area; the streets on either bank are busy and the water, when flowing, is uninviting. More appealing are the bathing beaches around the island (water rather muddy); the best is **Montjoly**. Bus B from the gare routière goes to Montjoly and Rémire, US$2.20, Monday-Saturday (last return from Montjoly 1840); Line 6 buses run from Cité Mirza, Cayenne (near Hotel Ket Taï) to Montjoly for beaches, US$2.20, Monday to Saturday. The last one returns about 1925, earlier at weekends (times vary). There is a walking trail called **Rorota** which follows the coastline and can be reached from Montjoly or the **Gosselin beaches**. Another trail, **Habitation Vidal** in Rémire, passes through former sugar cane plantations and ends at the remains of 19th-century sugar mills.

Some 43 km southwest of Cayenne is **Montsinéry**, with a nearby **zoo** ① *Macouria, T317306, www.zoodeguyane.com, daily 0930-1730, US$18, children US$11*, featuring Amazonian flora and fauna, a walking trail, canopy walkway, zip-line and other activities. To get there, take bus E from Place du Marché, US$5.50.

Outside Cayenne

space exploration, prison camps and wildlife-rich marshes

The European space centre at Kourou is one of the main attractions, especially when a rocket is being launched. In stark contrast are the abandoned penal settlements. Beyond is largely unexplored jungle. Also in this section are the routes to Suriname and Brazil.

West to Suriname
Kourou This is where the main French space centre (**Centre Spatial Guyanais**), used for the European Space Agency's Ariane programme, is located, 56 km southwest from Cayenne. It is also used by the Russians to launch Soyuz and

Essential Kourou

Finding your feet

There is no public transport to the space station so you'll need to take a taxi or hitch.

Tourist information

1 avenue de l'Anse, front de mer, T329833, ot-kourou@orange.fr, Mon, Tue, Thu 0900-1400, 1500-1630, Wed, Fri 0900-1400.

Tours

Public guided tours of the space station are given Monday to Friday 0800 and 1300, arrive 30 minutes early. Tours last three hours, but are only in French; under eights are not admitted. Reservations should be made 48 hours in advance, T326123, visites.csg@cnes.fr, Monday to Thursday 0800-1200, 1300-1700, Friday 0800-1200. No tours during a launch or on the days before or after.

Vega (a joint mission with other European countries). The site employs about 1500 personnel, with 7000 related jobs. Tourist attractions include bathing, fishing, sporting and a variety of organized excursions.

The space centre occupies an area of about 750 sq km along 50 km of coast, bisected by the Kourou river.

The **Musée de l'Espace** ⓘ *T326123, Mon-Fri 0800-1800, Sat 1400-1800, US$7.60 (US$4.35 on Sat and for those visiting the space centre the same day, and groups of 20 or more), can be visited without reservation.* It has a small planetarium. To watch a launch you must apply on line at www.cnes-csg.fr; CNES at the **Centre Spatial Guyanais** will then send you an invitation if successful. You must present your invitation and ID to attend. Full details on the website. Alternatively, you can watch the launch for free, from 10 km, at **Montagne Carapa** at Pariacabo. Some launches are shown on a big screen in Cayenne and Sinnamary. Also see www.esa.int/Education and www.arianespace.com.

Iles du Salut The Iles du Salut (many visitors at weekends), opposite Kourou, include the **Ile Royale**, **Ile Saint-Joseph**, and **Ile du Diable**. They were the scene of the notorious convict settlement built in 1852; the last prisoners left in 1953. One of their most famous residents was Henri Charrière, who made a miraculous escape to Venezuela. He later recounted the horrors of the penal colony and his hair-raising escape attempts in his book *Papillon* (some say Charrière's book is a compilation of prisoners' stories). There is a museum in the **Commander's House** on Ile Royale; brochures for sale. The **Ile du Diable** (**Devil's Island**), a rocky islet almost inaccessible from the sea, was where political prisoners, including Alfred Dreyfus, were held (access to this island is strictly forbidden). You can see monkeys, agoutis, turtles, hummingbirds and macaws, and there are many coconut palms on Ile Royale. Paintings of prison life by François Lagrange (the inspiration for Dustin Hoffman's character in the film *Papillon*) are on show in the tiny church. Visit the children's graveyard, mental asylum and death cells. These are not always open, but the church is open daily. Conservation work is underway. Three guided tours in French are given weekly.

Sinnamary and St-Laurent du Maroni Between Kourou and Iracoubo, on the road west, to St-Laurent (N1), is **Sinnamary** (116 km from Cayenne, bus US$22.50, 1 hour 20 minutes, no bus Sunday, US$11.25 from Kourou), a pleasant town where Kali'na (Galibi) Amerindians at a mission make artificial flowers, for sale to tourists. Carvings and jewellery are on sale here. **Tourist information** ⓘ *28 rue Constantin Verderosa, T346883, 0730-1230 (1500-1800 Mon, Wed).* There are three- to five-day excursions up the Sinnamary river. Scarlet ibis can be seen in numbers on the Sinnamary estuary at **Iracoubo**. All vehicles have to stop at Iracoubo for a police identity check.

St-Laurent du Maroni, formerly a penal transportation camp, is now a quiet, spread-out town with a few colonial buildings, 250 km from Cayenne on the river Maroni, which borders Suriname. Market days are Wednesday and Saturday, 0700-1400. It can be visited as a long day tour from Cayenne if you hire a car, but note that everything closes for a long siesta. The old **Camp de Transportation** (the original penal centre) can be visited on a 1¼-hour **guided tour** ⓘ *T278596, Jul-Aug daily 0930, 1100, 1500, 1630, rest of year Mon 1500, 1630, Tue-Sat as Jul-Aug, Sun 0930, 1100, buy tickets from tourist office US$6.65*. There are also chilling guided tours of **Les Bagnes (prison camps)** ⓘ *same times as above, US$13.35, which includes and exhibition (open Tue-Sat 0900-1200, 1430-1730, Sun 0900-1230, closed Mon and holidays); see also www.bagne-st-jean.com*, on the **Camp de la Relégation** at St-Jean du Maroni. On the riverfront by the Camp de Transportation, the **Office du Tourisme** ⓘ *1 esplanade Laurent Baudin, 97320 St-Laurent du Maroni, T342398, www.ot-saintlaurentdumaroni.fr, Tue-Sat 0800-1200, 1430-1800, Mon 1430-1800, Sun and holidays 0830-1230, but Jul-Aug Mon-Fri 0800-1800, Sat 0800-1230, 1430-1800 (Sun opens 0830)*, has lots of helpful information, list of local events, bicycles for hire, free Wi-Fi for one hour, and information on Ariane rocket launches (and bus to view it). There is a pleasant short walk along the riverfront from the tourist office.

Border with Suriname The port, together with customs and immigration, is 2 km south of the centre of St-Laurent du Maroni. The offices close at 1900. Boats across the river to Albina, Suriname, leave from two places: the Bac car ferry is the official crossing; countless unofficial pirogues leave from a different dock nearby (see Transport, below, for details). Whatever craft you take, you must get your exit stamp from immigration at the Bac terminal. Likewise in Albina, where there are two docks, immigration is at the Bac terminal. There is no legal money exchange in St-Laurent, but there is an official cambio in Albina, **Imex**, outside the Bac terminal (see page 64). Otherwise, there is a **Banque BRED** ATM beside Hotel Star (nine blocks from the dock) for withdrawing euros, and other ATMs in the centre. You will need euros for the buses and taxis. **Surinamese consul** ⓘ *6 rue Victor Schoelcher, T344968, Mon-Fri 0900-1200, 1400-1600. In Cayenne: 3 avenue L Héder (see Cayenne map, page 76), T282160, cg.sme.cay@foreignaffairs.gov.sr, Mon-Fri 0900-1200*. At the Cayenne consulate, hand in your passport with €30 in cash (or €32 for a credit card, Carte Bleue), wait 25 minutes then pick up your tourist card (no onward flights or other documents asked for); English spoken. See Visas and immigration, page 116, for other information.

Around St-Laurent About 3 km from St-Laurent, along the Paul Isnard road, is **Saint-Maurice**, where you can visit the **rum distillery** ⓘ *T340909, www.rhumssaintmaurice.com, Mon-Fri 0730-1130*. At Km 73 on the same dirt road is access to **Voltaire Falls**, 1½ hours' walk from the road. Some 7 km south of St-Laurent on the road to St-Jean du Maroni is the Amerindian village of **Terre Rouge.** Several companies in St-Laurent offer half-day, full-day and longer trips by boat up the Maroni river (also see Maripasoula below).

Some 40 km north of St-Laurent du Maroni is **Mana**, a delightful town with rustic architecture near the coast (**tourist office** ⓘ *rues M Bastie et Javouhey, T278409, Mon-Sat 0800-1300, 1500-1800*).

Some 20 km west of Mana following the river along a single-track access road is **Les Hattes**, or **Yalimapo**, an Amerindian village. About 4 km further on is **Les Hattes beach** where leatherback and other turtles lay their eggs at night. The season runs from April to August with May/June peak. There is no public transport to Les Hattes and its beach, but hitching is possible at weekends; take food and water and mosquito repellent. The freshwater of the Maroni and Mana rivers makes sea bathing pleasant. It is very quiet during the week.

Awala Yalimapo (or **Aouara**), a Kali'na Amerindian village with hammock places, is 16 km west of Les Hattes. The Kali'na, formerly called Galibi, claim Carib heritage and organize a number of traditional events, such as the **Kali'na Games** in December. It also has a beach where marine turtles lay their eggs; they take about three hours over it. Take mosquito nets, hammock and insect repellent. Both turtle-nesting beaches are within the **Réserve Naturelle Amana** ⓘ *270 avenue de 31 décembre 1988, 97319 Awala Yalimapo, T348404, amana2@wanadoo.fr, also on Facebook*, 14,800 ha of coastal and estuarine habitat protecting birds, both South American and migrants, mammals and reptiles. For more details see www. reserves-naturelles.org/amana and www.guyane-parcregional.fr/les-reserves-naturelles/reserve-naturelle-nationale-amana/.

There are daily flights from Cayenne to **Maripasoula**; details in Air transport, page 89, local office T372141. It is up the Maroni from St-Laurent (about four days' journey up river in a *pirogue*). There may be freight canoes that take passengers or private boats from St-Laurent (ask at the St-Laurent tourist office, see above, or see its website for names of operators); also four-day tours with **Guyane**-Évasion or other Cayenne operators. **Tourist office** ⓘ *Passage Vignon, T371509, www. maripasoula.fr, Mon 0900-1300, Tue-Sat 0900-1300, 1500-1700.*

South to Brazil
Some 6 km past the airport, route D6 turns off the main road to the east, N2, to the small town of **Roura**, about 28 km southeast of Cayenne (bus D, US$5.50 from gare routière in Cayenne). It has an interesting church. The road crosses a bridge at **Stoupan** over the Mahury river. Just outside Roura is the Laotian village of **Dacc**a, by the Crique Gabriel, a tributary of the Mahury. This is one of the main starting points for boat trips to the coast and island nature reserves of **Grand Connétable** (www.reserve-connetable.com) and **Ilet la Mère** and trips by pirogue inland to the **Fourgassier** (or **Fourgassié**) **Falls** (12 km away by road in the dry season), and further still along the Comté river to **Cacao**. See, for instance, www. yatoutatou.com or www.waykivillage.fr for trips, and prices. They also serve food, rent hammock spaces and canoes (US$22 per day for one), as does **Rour'Attitude** (http://amazonie-decouverte.com), an ecolodge near Roura ($$$$-$$$), which offers SUP, kayaks and other craft. For information about the area contact the **Roura tourist office** ⓘ *rue Georges Edmée Labrador, T270827, communication@ roura.gf and visit the www.guyane-amazonie.fr pages.*

From Roura, the paved D6 runs southeast towards the village of **Kaw** (bus D, US$7.15 from Roura), on an island amid swamps which are home to much rare wildlife including black caimans and birds such as hoatzin and, in the Kaw estuary, scarlet ibis. There are basic rooms available, but most visits are on tours locally (see www.richeandkaw.fr, www.guyane-tourisme973.com or www.lemorpho.com, among others) or from Cayenne, staying on houseboats. Take insect repellent. The

Réserve Naturelle Nationale Kaw-Roura, 94,700 ha, is administered by the Parc Naturel Régional de la Guyane ⓘ *www.guyane-parcregional.fr*.

At Km 53 on the main road southeast (N2) to Régina is the turn-off to **Cacao** (a further 13 km), a small, quiet village, where Hmong refugees from Laos are settled; they are farmers and produce fine traditional handicrafts. The Sunday morning market has local produce, Laotian food and embroidery (Sunday tours by boat with **JAL-Voyages** and Yatoutatou/Wayki Village – see above – US$50). Ask the **Comité du Tourisme de la Guyane** for gîtes and river trips in the area.

Régina, on the Approuague river southwest of Kaw, is reached by the paved N2 road from Cayenne. The Service Tourisme de Régina-Kaw is on rue Gaston Monnerville in Régina, T280589, or you can ask for information at the Mairie in Régina. A good two- to three-day trip is on the river to the Athanase falls (US$260-300 with Jal-Voyages); see also www.escapade-carbet.com/carbet/village-de-saut-athanase/. The road continues paved from Régina to **St-Georges de l'Oyapock** (difficult in the rainy season).

Saül This remote gold-mining settlement in the 'massif central' is the geographical centre of Guyane. The main attractions are for the nature-loving tourist. Beautiful undisturbed tropical forests are accessible by a very well-maintained system of some 75 km of marked trails, including several circular routes. There is running water and electricity; the tourist office is in the town hall. There are a couple of places to stay and eat in town (see **A Ke Nou**, http://gite-restaurantakenou-saul.com, and **Chez Lulu**, www.chezlulu-saul.com, for example). Two markets sell food.

Saül and Maripasoula (see above) are within the contact zone (*zone d'adhésion*) of the **Parc Amazonien de Guyane** which covers two million hectares of the interior, almost the entire southern half of the country from the rivers Oyapock to the Maroni. Together with neighbouring reserves in Brazil such as Tumucumaque, Maricuru and Grão-Pará, this forms the world's largest protected tropical forest and is one of the planet's most biodiverse regions. According the French national parks website, www.parcsnationaux.fr, the Parc Amazonien contains 192 species of mammal, 261 species of reptile and amphibian, 400 species of freshwater fish, 719 species of bird and some 1500 types of tree. It is also home to five indigenous groups and one maroon community. Access is "difficile".

St-Georges de l'Oyapock This small town, with its small detachment of the French Foreign Legion who parade on **Bastille Day**, is 15 minutes downriver from Oiapoque in Brazil, €5/US$5.50 per person by motorized canoe, bargain for a return fare. A bridge between the two countries was completed in 2011, but remains closed until various infrastructure projects on the Brazilian side are finished. Ask in the Mairie, rue Jean Cedia, T370997, for **tourist information**. There are bars, restaurants, supermarkets with French specialities, a post office and public telephones which take phonecards. **Oyapock Évasion** ⓘ *T272683 or mobiles T694-961961 or T694-946962, www.oyapock-evasion.com*, offers guided river and forest tours, trips to Brazil and transport. A day trip can be made to the **Saut Maripa rapids** (not very impressive with high water, but strewn with treacherous rocks), located about 30 minutes upstream along the Oyapock river, past the Brazilian towns of Oiapoque and Clevelândia do Norte. Hire a motorized *pirogue* (canoe) to take you to a landing downstream from the rapids. Then walk along the trolley track (used to move heavy goods around the rapids) for 20 minutes. In dry season 4WDs can get there. There are more rapids further upstream on the way to and beyond Camopi.

Border with Brazil For entry/exit stamps, look for PAF (**Police Federal**), set away from the river about 10 minutes' walk behind the Mairie; fork left at 'Farewell Greeting' sign from town (this may change when the border bridge is in service). Open daily 0700-1200, 1500-1800 (often not open after early morning on Sunday, so try police at the airport); French, Portuguese and English spoken. The **Brazilian consulate** in Cayenne is at 444 chemin St Antoine, T296010, cg.caiena@ itamaraty.gov.br, Monday-Friday 0730-1300, 1330-1500. One of the **Livre Service** supermarkets and **Hotel Chez Modestine** will sometimes change dollars cash into euros at poor rates; if entering the country here, change money before arriving in St-Georges. Brazilian reais are accepted in shops at poor rates.

Listings Guyane *map page 76.*

Tourist information

Cayenne

Comité du Tourisme de la Guyane
12 rue Lallouette, BP 801, 97300 Cayenne, T296500, www.guyane-amazonie.fr. Mon, Wed, Fri 0730-1330, Tue, Thu 0730-1300, 1400-1700.
Helpful and has lots of brochures, but little in English. The tourist office app is www.guyane-amazonie.fr/application-mobile. Cayenne also has a **municipal tourist office** (12 rue Louis Blanc, T396883, www.ville-cayenne.fr/ a-la-decouverte-de-cayenne/Mon-Fri 0830-1200, 1400-1700, Sat 0830-1300).

Where to stay

Cayenne
Most hotels are in the centre. A few of the better ones are in the suburb of Montjoly. Most hotels have to add a small municipal tax to the bill: it is charged daily, per person and varies from hotel to hotel. Service is rarely added to the bill. Hotels rarely include breakfast in the price either, but B&B accommodation with breakfast (gîte) is available from €45/US$50 a night. Apartment rental is another good option, but what's on offer changes often. The tourist office's web page lists what is available in all categories, with full details and pictures, www.guyane-amazonie.fr/se-loger.

$$$$ Ker Alberte
4 rue de Docteur Sainte-Rose, T257570, www.hotelkeralberte.com.
Lovely hotel in a converted old house in the heart of the city, the courtyard pool area has rooms behind and above it, also 3 rooms in the older villa, 3 standards of room, the best have a terrace, some with kitchen, good service, decorated with

modern art, restaurant with daily lunch menu (**$$$**), café and tapas bar.

$$$$-$$$ Best Western Amazonia
28 Av Général de Gaulle, T288300, www.hotel-amazonia.com.
A/c rooms in 4 categories, pool, central location, good buffet breakfast extra, also buffet lunch, dinner à la carte in **L'Outre-mer** restaurant.

$$$$-$$$ Hotel des Palmistes
12 Av Général de Gaulle, T300050, www.palmistes.com.
Fine hotel in a 19th-century building with comfortable rooms and suites overlooking the Place des Palmistes. Restaurant (**$$$**) is open 7 days a week for all meals, good food, music at weekends, also has a popular bar for cocktails and people-watching.

$$$$-$$$ Le Dronmi
42 Av Général de Gaulle, T317770, www.ledronmi.com.
Spacious suites on 2 floors with kitchen, also smaller rooms with microwave, free use of washing machine in the daytime, helpful staff and secure entrance, but keys held behind the bar at **Le Bistro**, downstairs, where breakfast (included in price) is served, as well as other meals; there's also a popular bar.

$$$ Central Hotel
Corner rue Molé and rue Becker, T256565, www.centralhotel-cayenne.fr.
Good location, 2½ blocks from the Place de Palmistes, a/c rooms. Special prices at weekends. **Bar François** on 1st floor. Book in advance online.

$$$ Hotel des Amandiers
Place Auguste-Horth, T289728, www.hoteldesamandiers.com.
Pleasant, tranquil and breezy location across from the Place des Amandiers, a/c

rooms, cheapest on ground floor, most expensive with sea view. Also has a café which serves breakfast and is open all day for drinks, good service.

$$$ La Belle Étoile and Villa Soleil
74 rue Lt Goinet, T257085, www.prestigelocations.fr.
The first is a brand new building with 6 deluxe suites on 3 floors, while the latter is the ground floor of a Creole villa, quaint, old style. All suites with kitchen, safe, a/c, washing machine. Very good. In the same group is **Éclipse**, 47 rue Lt Goinet, same phone, website and price.

$$$-$$ Ket Taï
72 Av Nelson Mandela, T289777, g.chang@wanadoo.fr.
The best cheap hotel in town, by the canal at the corner of the central area, simple a/c rooms, en suites. If you can, look at a few rooms before deciding.

Around Rémire-Montjoly

$$$ Motel du Lac
22 rue Poupon, Route de Montjoly, T380800, moteldulac@orange.fr.
In a protected area, very peaceful, garden, pool, bar, restaurant.

Near Matoury and the airport

$$$ La Chaumière
Chemin de la Chaumière (off the road to Kourou), 97351 Matoury, T255701, www.lachaumierecayenne.com.
Set in gardens, rooms, bungalows, a studio and a villa, restaurant, pool, at bottom end of this price band, good value, but cabs to town push up cost.

Kourou
Hotel rooms and rates are at a premium when there's an Ariane rocket launch (once a month).

$$$$ Hôtel des Roches
Av des Roches, T320066,
www.hoteldesroches.com.
Fair, a/c, includes breakfast, pool with bar,
Le Paradisier and **Le Créolia** restaurants,
buffet breakfast included, Wi-Fi.

$$$$ Mercure Ariatel
Av de St-Exupéry, Lac Bois Diable,
T328900, www.accorhotels.com.
Overlooking a lake, 9-hole golf course
nearby and pool. Has **Snack Ti Gourmet**
for grills and salads and **Mahogany Bar**.

$$$$-$$$ Atlantis
Lieu dit Bois Diable, T321300,
www.atlantiskourou.com.
A/c, modern, pool, best value for
business visitors.

$$$-$$ Le Ballahou
1 et 3 rue Amet Martial, T220022,
www.hotel-ballahou.com.
Small apart-hotel, some rooms with
cooking facilities, also studios, a/c, TV,
modern, massage and other therapies.
Book ahead.

Iles du Salut

$$$$-$$$ Auberge Iles du Salut
Ile Royale (BP 324, 97310 Kourou,
T321100, sothis2@wanadoo.fr).
Full board. 60-bed hotel, hammock space
(US$11); former guard's bungalow (**$$$**),
main meals are excellent; pricey gift shop
(especially when cruise ship is in).

Sinnamary

$$$ Hôtel du Fleuve
11 rue Léon Mine, T345400,
infohoteldufleuve@orange.fr.
On the main highway, by the roundabout
into Sinnamary, with gardens, restaurant,
internet access, pool, one of the grandest
hotels west of Cayenne, breakfast extra.

St-Laurent du Maroni

$$$$-$$$ Le Relais des 3 Lacs
19-21 allée des Toucans, T340505,
reservationr3l@yahoo.fr.
Bungalows with kitchen, studios and
rooms, a/c, shuttle to town centre,
restaurant, gardens, pool.

$$$ Amazonia du Fleuve
20 rue Thiers, T341010,
hotelamazonia@orange.fr.
Quite smart, Wi-Fi, safe in rooms,
buffet breakfast.

$$$ La Tentiaire
12 av Franklin Roosevelt, T342600,
tentiaire@wanadoo.fr.
A/c, the best, breakfast extra, phone,
pool, secure parking. Will only accept
reservations if you phone credit card
details through in advance (not always
possible), will not hold rooms. If full, they
will ring round other hotels.

$$$ Star
26 bis rue Thiers, T341084,
hotelstar973@yahoo.fr.
A bit cavernous, functional, white-
tiled rooms, a/c, Wi-Fi not always
available in rooms, safe in more
expensive rooms, pool.

$$ Chez Julienne
Rue Gaston Monnerville, 200 m past
Texaco station, some way out of town
on main road, T341153.
A/c, TV, a/c, shower, good value.

Around St-Laurent
The following gîtes are all at **Commune
Awala-Yalimapo** (http://awala-yalimapo.
mairies-guyane.org): **Ailumi Weyulu**
(T347245, www.giteailumiweyulu.com);
Chez Rita (Awala, T344914, gitechezrita@
gmail.com); **Kudawyada** (260 av du
31 décembre 1988, T342060). Shared

accommodation: **Auberge de Jeunesse Simili** (T341625, ajs.simili@wanadoo.fr).

$$$$-$$$ Auberge des Chutes Voltaires
Voltaire Falls, www.aubergechutes voltaire.com.
Price is for half-board. Double rooms with bath or shared bath, hammock space US$66 half-board, US$11 to hire hammock (more with mosquito net), other meals available.

South to Brazil

$$ Auberge des Orpailleurs
8 km after the Cacao turn-off on the road from Cayenne to Régina, by the Orapu river, T0970-447855 (net phone), www.aubergedesorpailleurs.com.
6 rooms and also hammock spaces, breakfast extra. Canoes, trails and butterfly and moth collecting. Restaurant.

$$ Auberge de l'Approuague
Lieu-dit Corossony, 97390 Régina, T0694-446979, www.approuague.com.
Price is for double room, hammock space costs US$17.25, cheaper with own hammock, a 3-course meals costs US$27, great views of the forest.

$$-$ Auberge du Camp Caïman
Route D6, 29 km from Roura, T307277.
Tourist camp (much less to hang a hammock), tours arranged to watch caiman in the swamps.

Border with Brazil: St-Georges de l'Oyapock
Accommodation is cheaper on the Brazilian side.

$$$ Chez Modestine
Rue E Elfort, on the main square, T370013, modestine@wanadoo.fr.
A/c or fan, rooms in a traditional house, Wi-Fi, restaurant.

$$ Caz Cale
Rue E Elfort, 1st back from riverfront, just east of the main square, T370054.
A/c rooms with TV, cheaper with fan.

Restaurants

Cayenne
Many restaurants close on Sun. There are several small Chinese restaurants serving the same fare: noodles, rice, soups, etc.

$$$ La Marina
24 bis rue Molé, T301930. Open 1145-1430, 1900-2230, closed Sun.
Mainly for seafood, but also beef and chicken dishes. Next door is **La Taverne** (No 26, T290466, open 1200-1430, 1900-2230), with a general menu, cassoulet a speciality, and next door again is **La Perle d'Asie** (T291609), Chinese, cheaper than the other 2.

$$$ La Petite Maison
23 rue Féliz Eboué, T385839, www. restaurantlapetitemaison.com. Mon-Sat 1200-1400, 2000-2200.
In an old building, on 2 floors, with a good varied menu.

$$$ Le Patriarche
12 rue Samuel Lubin, T317644.
Excellent classical French and Creole cooking, one of the best in Guyane and very good value for this country. Reserve in advance.

$$$ Paris-Cayenne
59 rue de Lallouette, T317617, www.pariscayenne.fr.
French cooking with tropical twist, also with bar, nice decor.

$$$-$$ Café de la Gare
42 rue Léopold Héder, T285320.
Great little restaurant with club playing classy live music every Thu and

weekend. Good atmosphere, 20- to 40-something crowd.

$$$-$$ Le Café Crème
42 rue Justin Catayée, T281256.
Pastries, sandwiches, juices and coffee; open for breakfast and lunch only, friendly.

$$$-$$ Mille Pâtes
52 rue J Catayée, T289180, www.mille pates-guyane.com. Daily 1130-2230 (2300 Fri, Sat and night before a holiday). Other branches open 1145-1430, 1900-2230.
Meat and fish dishes (a board tells you where each cut of meat is from), mixed menu of pizza, pasta, burgers and daily specials, also take-away and delivery, a little English spoken.

$$ Nath, Café, Thé & Go
33 rue J Catayée.
Lots of coffees, teas, smoothies and cakes. Pleasant.

Kourou

$$$-$$ Le P'tit Café
11 Place Monnerville, T326856.
A good value set lunch and a respectable à la carte menu.

$ Chinatown
66 rue Duchesne.
Cheap Chinese (also takeaway). Recommended.

$ Le Glacier des 2 Lacs
68 Av des 2 Lacs, T321210.
Ice cream, cakes, teas, very good.

St-Laurent du Maroni

$$$ La Goelette
Balaté Plage, 2.5 km from St-Laurent, T342897, lagoelette.restaurant@ orange.fr. Tue-Sun 1200-1400, 1830-2100.

In a converted fishing boat on the river, serving fish and game. Nice atmosphere in the evenings. In the same group as **Greenheart Hotel** (www.greenheart-hotel.com) and **Guesthouse Un Pied-à-Terre** (http://guesthouse-un-pied-a-terre.com) in Paramaribo.

$$$ Ti Pic Kréol's
24 rue Thiers (next to Star Hotel), T340983, www.tipickreols.com. Restaurant 1200-1430, 1900-2200, bar open all the time, closed Sun evening.
Excellent restaurant/bar, Créole menu including local game, popular for lunch, good service, pool table. Recommended.

$$ Le Mambari
7 rue Rousseau, T343590. Open till late.
French cuisine using local ingredients served in a traditional building.

Shopping

Cayenne
Bookshops
La Case A Bulles, *51 rue du Lieutenant Goinet, www.kazabul.com.*

What to do

Cayenne
Look under **Espace Pro** on www.guyane-amazonie.fr for listings of local tour operators. Pick-ups from the airport and accommodation in Cayenne for a night or 2 are usually part of the package. Full details on the company websites, some in English.
Guyane-Évasion, *ZI Degrad des Cannes, Montjoly, T294164, info@guyane-evasion.com, or see Facebook.* New company in 2016 offering day trips (2 to 5 days), river trips, visits to tourist camps and longer excursions to the interior.
JAL-Voyages, *26 Av Général de Gaulle, T316820, www.jal-voyages.com.* Range

of river tours, eg on the Approuague (US$220), on a houseboat on the Kaw marshes (from US$90 for day visit to US$175 for day and night, full board, including transport from Cayenne, very good accommodation, food and birdwatching), Amerindian villages, the Grand Connétable bird reserve and Ilet la Mère and Devil's Island, little English spoken. Recommended.

Transport

Cayenne
Air
Cayenne Airport – Félix Éboué (T353882/89) 17 km south of Cayenne. There is a virtual tourist office with direct phone and an information office with little information. Bars, cafés, car hire and an ATM for Visa and Mastercard. Transfer by taxi; they wait outside and use meters (a card shows the rates per metre): US$35 to town by day, US$50 at night and on Sun, 20 mins. 67 km from Kourou (US$55-70). Cheapest route to town is taxi to Concorde, then bus F to gare routière in the centre US$3.65 (every 1 hr 15 mins, 0655-1855, far fewer on Sat, none on Sun), or taxi to **Matoury** US$10, then bus C, US$2 (more frequent service, none on Sun). Cheapest return to airport is by bus C to Matoury, or F to Concorde, then hitch or walk.

Bus
Regular local services run by **SMTC**, most from the Place du Marché, US$1.20 (ticket office 2682 route de la Madeleine, T254929, Mon-Fri 0800-1200, 1500-1700; see www.ville-cayenne.fr/transports-lignes-horaires-tarifs/ – has maps). Interurban terminal, Gare routière is at corner of rue Molé and Av de la Liberté. To **St-Laurent du Maroni**, direct minibuses, 3¼ hrs, US$38, leaves when full from the opposite side of the canal from gare routière, or a bigger bus at 0800, 1100, 1300, 1500 via Kourou and Iracoubo US$27.50. To **St-Georges del' Oyapock**, US$44 (with Didier, T0694-437851, Dudu, T916998, Marcio, T130040), or US$33.50 via **Régina** (US$22.50, 1½ hrs, Cayenne-Régina, US$11 Régina-St-Georges).

Shared taxi (*collectifs*) From the gare routière, corner of Av de la Liberté and rue Malouet by the Canal Laussat, early morning, ask around as they are not signed; a bit more expensive than buses. They leave when full. Other taxis at the stand on Place des Palmistes, corner of Av Gen de Gaulle and Molé.

Car hire
There are 11 agencies in Cayenne; those at the airport open only for flight arrivals. **Avis** (www.avis.fr), **Hertz** (www.hertzantilles.com) and **Ucar** (www.ucar-guyane.com). **Budget** (www.budget-guyane.com), **Europcar** (http://en.europcar-guyane.com) and **Sixt** (www.sixt.com) have offices. All types of car available. Cheapest rates are about €40/US$45 a day, km and insurance extra. Check insurance details carefully; the excess is very high.

Kourou
Bus
To/from **Cayenne**, US$11. To **St-Laurent du Maroni**, US$27.

Taxi
Shared taxi to **Cayenne**, US$16. Taxi to Cayenne or airport, US$90, more at night. To **St-Laurent du Maroni** US$30 by *taxi collectif* (irregular).

Iles du Salut
Boat
Sailing boats and motorboats go from Kourou to the islands: *Iles du Salut* catamaran, 100 passengers, from Ponton des Boulourous in Kourou, T284236, www.promaritimeguyane.fr, at 0830 daily, return at 1630 (embark 45 mins before departure), US$46.25 return, children under 12 US$24, 1 hr each way (book in advance online). The 12-seater *St Joseph* sails between Ile Royale and Ile Saint-Joseph, weather permitting, for US$6. Tickets may be obtained direct or from agencies in Cayenne or Kourou. Catamarans such as *Tropic-Alizés* (T0694-402020, www. ilesdusalut-guyane.com) and *La Hulotte* (T323381, www.lahulotte-guyane.fr) run sailing excursions to the islands, US$55 for a full day; 2-day trips also offered. No sailings between Ile Royale and Ile du Diable.

St-Laurent du Maroni and around
Air
Service with **Air Guyane** from **Cayenne**, daily, US$95. **Air Guyane** flies from Cayenne to **Maripasoula**, daily, 1 hr, US$99; minibus airport to town US$5.50, awaits flight arrival. See page 81 for information on river transport to Maripasoula.

Bus
To **Cayenne, Transports Best**, T341400, 0600, from St-Laurent gare routière, US$27.50. Minibuses meet the ferry from Suriname, leaving when full from rue du Port, 3 hrs, US$38. If none direct, change in **Iracoubo**. To **Mana** and Awala with **Van Els,** T0694-236602, 4 daily, 2 on Sun, US$10. To **Kourou**, Antoinette et Frères from La Glacière, T0694-167322, US$27.50. There are several *taxis collectifs* (US$38 to Cayenne from gare routière, plus US$6 for hotel pick-up) and regular taxis; tourist office has phone numbers.

Border with Suriname
Boat
The vehicle and passenger ferry to **Albina,** Bac International *La Gabrielle* (T279129, bac.gabrielle@orange.fr), has 3-4 crossings a day, 6 on Sat, 30 mins. Passengers US$5 one way, car US$36.75, payable only in euros. Service can change at any time. This is the official crossing. Countless unofficial pirogues cross from a different port nearby, US$5 (or US$10.75 for 1 person). See page 80 for immigration details.

Minibus and taxi
Transport to/from **Paramaribo** meets the Albina ferry.

South to Brazil
Air
Service with **Air Guyane** from Cayenne to Saül, daily except Sat, US$82. Try airport even if flight full.

Minibus
From Cayenne to **Cacao**, Mon-Fri 0725, 1600, return Mon-Fri 0600, 1725, US$18.

St-Georges de l'Oyapock
Minibus
To **Cayenne**, price and schedule as above, or change in Régina. Buses to **Macapá** leave late afternoon, 10 hrs: book when you arrive in Oiapoque (Brazilian side).

Background

Pre-Columbian history

Archaeological research in what is now the Guianas concentrates on the whole geographical region bounded by the Atlantic Ocean, the rivers Orinoco, Amazon and Negro and the Casiquiare Canal, the natural waterway that links the Negro and Orinoco. Compared with other parts of South America investigations are at a relatively early stage, but evidence suggests that the area was populated by groups who employed a variety of subsistence strategies. From the earliest nomadic hunters of large animals roaming the savannahs in the late Pleistocene (which ended 11,700 years ago) to the first millennium AD, the pattern appears to be of a hunting, gathering and fishing lifestyle, seldom settled in one place and lacking the type of complex structures found on South America's Pacific coast or in the Andes. It would appear that two main cultural groups began to develop before 900 AD, with present-day Cayenne marking the division between them. The western peoples spread from the Orinoco to the coast of the Guianas and occupied the sandy ridges or built mounds for their villages above the swampy coastal plain. They also built an extensive system of raised fields for their crops. East of Cayenne, the people spread up from the Amazon into Amapá (Brazil) and Guyane, with a major settlement area in the hills between the Oiapoque/Oyapok and Ouanary rivers. Their polychrome pottery, funerary customs, megaliths and village and rock-shelter habitations set them apart from the western group. It was these peoples who witnessed the arrival of the Europeans in the late 15th century.

On his third voyage to the Americas in 1498, Columbus' exploration of the Orinoco delta led him to conclude that he had reached a great continent. Subsequent European voyagers touched upon the northeast coast of South America but attempts at settlement were few and far between, thwarted by aggressive indigenous people, disease and isolation. As understanding of the continent and its riches grew and as Spain and Portugal conquered large swathes of the land, the Wild Coast between the Orinoco and the Amazon became more of a lure, in part because it was rumoured to be a possible route to the fabled and as-yet undiscovered city of El Dorado, but also a possible foothold in South America to break the Iberian domination. On both counts Sir Walter Ralegh (or Raleigh) was instrumental, but not alone, in fuelling these ambitions. His expedition of 1595 and its description in *The Discoverie of the Large, Rich and Bewtiful Empyre of Guiana* published in 1596 captured the imagination. The coast was mapped and English, French and Dutch explorers, traders and hopeful settlers arrived.

Guyana The country was first partially settled between 1616 and 1621 by the Dutch West India Company, who erected a fort and depot at Fort Kyk-over-al (County of Essequibo). The first English attempt at settlement was made by Captain Leigh on the Oiapoque River (now French Guyane) in 1604, but he failed to establish a permanent settlement. Lord Willoughby founded a settlement in 1663 at Suriname, which was captured by the Dutch in 1667 and ceded to them at the Peace of Breda in exchange for New York. The Dutch held the three colonies till 1796 when they were captured by a British fleet. The territory was restored to the Dutch in 1802, but in the following year was retaken by Great Britain, which finally gained it in 1814, when the counties of Essequibo, Berbice and Demerara were merged to form British Guiana.

During the 17th century the Dutch and English settlers established posts upriver, in the hills, mostly as trading points with the Amerindian natives. Plantations were laid out and worked by African slaves. Poor soil defeated this venture, and the settlers retreated with their slaves to the coastal area in mid-18th century: the old plantation sites can still be detected from the air. Coffee and cotton were the main crops until the late 18th century, but sugar had become the dominant crop by 1820. In 1834 slavery was abolished. Many slaves became small landholders, and settlers had to find another source of labour: indentured workers from India, a few Chinese, and some Portuguese labourers. At the end of their indentures many settled in Guyana.

The end of the colonial period was politically turbulent, with rioting between the mainly Indo-Guyanese People's Progressive Party (PPP), led by Dr Cheddi Jagan, and the mainly Afro-Guyanese People's National Congress (PNC), under Mr Forbes Burnham. The PNC, favoured over the PPP by the colonial authorities, formed a government in 1964 and retained office until 1992. Guyana is one of the few countries in the Caribbean where political parties have used race as an election issue. As a result, tension between the ethnic groups has manifested itself mainly at election time.

On 26 May 1966 Guyana gained independence, and on 23 February 1970 it became a co-operative republic within the Commonwealth. The constitution of 1980 declared Guyana to be in transition from capitalism to socialism and relations with the USSR and Eastern Europe were fostered. Following the death of President Forbes Burnham in August 1985, Desmond Hoyte became president, since when relations with the United States improved.

Regular elections to the National Assembly and to the presidency since independence were widely criticized as fraudulent. In October 1992 national assembly and presidential elections, declared free and fair by international observers, the PPP/Civic party, led by Dr Jagan, won power after 28 years in opposition. The installation of a government by democratic means was greeted with optimism, including by foreign investors and the IMF.

In March 1997, President Jagan died after a heart attack. In elections on 15 December 1997, the PPP/C alliance was re-elected with Jagan's widow, Janet, as president. Desmond Hoyte and the PNC disputed the results and a brief period of violent demonstrations was ended by mediation from Caricom, the Caribbean Common Market. Even though the PPP/C was sworn in to office on 24 December 1997, agreeing to review the constitution and hold new elections within three years, Hoyte refused to recognize Jagan as president. In August 1999 President Jagan resigned because of ill health and Minister of Finance, Bharrat Jagdeo was appointed in her place. In subsequent elections in March 2001 the PPP/C alliance and Jagdeo were returned to office. After the death of Desmond Hoyte in December 2002, his succcessor Robert Corbin agreed terms with Jagdeo which included an end to the PNC/Reform's boycott of the National Assembly. Jagdeo and the PPP/C again won elections on 28 August 2006, but this time without the inter-party violence that had marred previous polls. This, plus the good showing of the new Alliance for Change (AFC), which campaigned on a non-racial platform, raised hopes for better relations within Guyana's racially divided society.

In the elections of November 2011, PPP/C won the most seats in parliament and its candidate, Donald Ramotar, was named president. PPP/C failed by one seat to win an outright majority, though, as A Partnership for National Unity (APNU – a coalition of PNC and several smaller parties) gained 26 seats and AFC seven to PPP/C's 32. The opposition used its one-seat advantage to delay and thwart legislation and to impose spending cuts. The president refused to implement the cuts; the assembly passed a motion of no confidence and, in November 2014, Ramotar suspended parliament. In January 2015 he called for early elections which were held on 11 May and were won by the APNU/AFC alliance with the same 33- to 32-seat majority as before. David Grainger of APNU was sworn in as president.

An early challenge for the Grainger administration was Venezuela's claim to sovereignty over the territorial waters off the Essequibo Region. Guyana called the annexation of the continental shelf a violation of international law. Venezuela had objected that Guyana should not grant concessions for oil exploration in the disputed waters to US company Exxon-Mobil who, in both 2015 and 2016, announced the discovery of significant deposits. The argument continued in 2016 and before leaving office in December 2016 UN Secretary General Ban Ki-Moon gave the two countries one year to resolve their territorial dispute. If they fail, the UN will hand the case over to the International Court of Justice.

Since 2009 Guyana has subscribed to an Avoided Deforestation (AD) initiative aimed at setting its rainforest under long-term protection in return for international compensation and support for sustainable development. One casualty of the 2014 political impasse (see above) was a bill to facilitate loans for a hydroelectric scheme at Amaila Falls, which was viewed as essential to provide cheap power for the country. The US developer pulled out of the project and the government declared it 'dead'. But because the Amaila Falls project is a key part of Guyana's Low Carbon Development Strategy and is linked to the AD initiative, an effect of the stalemate was that Norway withheld a US$40 million tranche of its support for AD until the APNU government made its position clear on the Strategy. As of June 2015 Norway had committed US$190 million to the US$250 million for AD, but of that sum the majority (84%) remained in accounts with the World and Inter-American Development Banks awaiting disbursement. By January 2017 no decision had been taken on Amaila, but the government did announce that it wished to set up a green energy fund, using US$80 million deposited by Norway in the IADB, to finance other renewable energy projects.

Linked to the plan to keep the rainforest intact is the growing popularity of Guyana as an ecotourism destination. Ecotourism, however, remains a small part of Guyana's tourism mix. In 2012 tourism arrivals rose by almost 20% to about 150,000, the majority being people of Guyanese descent returning for their holidays and the majority of those coming from the US. New measurements for arrivals were introduced by the Caribbean Tourism Organization in 2013 so direct comparisons cannot be made, but in 2014 arrivals were 205,824, and in 2015 206,800. In the nine months to September 2016, arrivals were 170,318, an increase of 11% over the previous year, largely because of the celebrations for 50 years of independence.

Guyane Several French and Dutch expeditions attempted to settle along the coast in the early 17th century, but were driven off by the native population. The French finally established a settlement at Sinnamary in the early 1660s but this was destroyed by the Dutch in 1665 and seized by the British two years later. Under the Treaty of Breda, 1667, Guyane was returned to France. Apart from a brief occupation by the Dutch in 1676, it remained in French hands until 1809 when a combined Anglo-Portuguese naval force captured the colony and handed it over to the Portuguese (Brazilians). Though the land was restored to France by the Treaty of Paris in 1814, the Portuguese remained until 1817. Gold was discovered in 1853, and disputes arose about the frontiers of the colony with Suriname and Brazil. These were settled by arbitration in 1891, 1899, and 1915. The colony was used as a prison for French convicts with camps scattered throughout the country; Saint-Laurent was the port of entry. After serving prison terms convicts spent an equal number of years in exile and were usually unable to earn their return passage to France. By the law of 19 March 1946, the Colony of Cayenne, or Guyane Française, became the Department of Guyane, with the same laws, regulations, and administration as a department in metropolitan France. The seat of the Prefect and of the principal courts is at Cayenne. A small minority, represented by the MDES (Decolonization and Social Emancipation Movement), favours independence, but in a referendum in 2010 the majority of voters rejected greater autonomy. The French government has made no move to alter the department's status. Council elections were held in December 2015, when a new Collectivité Territoriale Unique with 51 seats, uniting the General and Regional councils, was formed. Despite heavy dependence economically on France, unemployment and a rapidly expanding population are seen as a serious problem. Local politicians have called for greater investment from France to prevent the department falling into underdevelopment. A second problem is illegal immigration, in part by gold prospectors, whom the French government has tried to evict in several campaigns. The loss of Guyane's largely untouched rainforest to illicit mining is currently small, but potentially significant. Another source of illegal immigration was Haiti with, in mid-2016, a reported 4000 asylum applications from all countries pending. According to the tourist authorities, Guyane received some 220,000 visitors in 2015, of whom 48% were business travellers and 33% were visiting relatives or friends. Just over 40% went to the Centre Spatial at Kourou.

Suriname Although Amsterdam merchants had been trading with the Wild Coast of Guiana as early as 1613 (the name Parmurbo-Paramaribo was already known) it was not until 1630 that 60 English settlers came to Suriname under Captain Marshall and planted tobacco. The real founder of the colony was Lord Willoughby of Parham, governor of Barbados, who sent an expedition to

Suriname in 1651 under Anthony Rous to find a suitable place for settlement. Willoughbyland became an agricultural colony with 500 little sugar plantations, 1000 white inhabitants and 2000 African slaves. Jews from Holland and Italy joined them, as well as Dutch Jews ejected from Brazil after 1654. On 27 February 1667, Admiral Crijnssen conquered the colony for the states of Zeeland and Willoughbyfort became the present Fort Zeelandia. By the Peace of Breda, 31 July 1667, it was agreed that Suriname should remain with the Netherlands, while Nieuw-Amsterdam (New York) should be given to England. The colony was conquered by the British in 1799, only to be restored to the Netherlands with the Treaty of Paris in 1814. Slavery was forbidden in 1818 and formally abolished in 1863. Indentured labour from China and Indonesia (Java) took its place.

On 25 November 1975, the country became an independent republic, which signed a treaty with the Netherlands for an economic aid programme worth US$1.5 billion until 1985. A military coup on 25 February 1980 overthrew the elected government. The military leader, Sergeant Desi Bouterse, and his associates came under pressure from the Dutch and the USA as a result of dictatorial tendencies. After the execution of 15 opposition leaders at Fort Zeelandia on 8 December 1982 (the December Murders), the Netherlands broke off relations and suspended its aid programme, although bridging finance was restored in 1988.

The ban on political parties was lifted in late 1985 and a new constitution was drafted. In 1986 guerrilla rebels (the Jungle Commando), led by a former bodyguard of the promoted Lieutenant-Colonel Bouterse, Ronny Brunswijk, mounted a campaign to overthrow the government, disrupting both plans for political change and the economy. Nevertheless, elections for the National Assembly were held in November 1987. A three-party coalition (the Front for Democracy and Development) gained a landslide victory over the military, but conflicts between Assembly President Ramsewak Shankar and Bouterse led to the deposition of the government in a bloodless coup on 24 December 1990 (the 'telephone coup'). A military-backed government under the presidency of Johan Kraag was installed and elections for a new national assembly were held on 25 May 1991. The New Front of three traditional parties and the Surinamese Labour Party (SPA) won most Assembly seats and Ronald Venetiaan was elected president on 6 September 1991. Meetings between Suriname and the Netherlands ministers after the 1991 elections led to the renewal of aid in 1992. In August 1992, a peace treaty was signed between the government and the Jungle Commando.

During the 1990s successive administrations, characterised by alliances and defections, tried to deal with a foundering economy. Throughout the manoeuvrings following the 1996 elections, Bouterse's National Democratic Party (NDP) played a greater or lesser role even if the leader himself did not hold a position of power. In fact at this time, in July 1999, Bouterse was convicted *in absentia* in the Netherlands on charges of drug trafficking. Elections in May 2000 were won by the New Front coalition led by ex-president Venetiaan. His most urgent priority was to stabilize the economy, which, by 2000 and with Dutch aid terminated, had fallen back into recession. From 2001, there were renewed signs of improvement, but the outlook remained grim for over 60% of the population estimated by the

United Nations to be living in poverty. In January 2004, Suriname abandoned its currency, the guilder, in favour of the Suriname dollar, and simplified exchange rates. In general elections in May 2005, the outgoing New Front coalition retained power, even though Bouterse's NDP became the largest single political party in the country. Five years later the NDP, with its Mega Coalition partners which included Ronny Brunswijk's A-Combination, overturned the NF's majority and in July 2010 parliament elected Bouterse as president, regardless of the convictions and accusations hanging over him. In April 2012 a law was passed giving the president and 24 other suspects amnesty from any alleged involvement in the December Murders. The decision outraged many, including the Dutch government, as did other pardons granted by Bouterse. On the other hand, Bouterse's son, Dino, was arrested in Panama and deported to the US on charges of drug-trafficking and attempting to set up a training facility for Hezbollah in Suriname. He pleaded guilty to the terrorism charge and was sentenced to 16 years in jail.

General elections were held on 25 May 2015 and the NDP won a slim outright majority. Second was the V7 coalition with 18 seats. Ronny Brunswijk's A-Combination won 5. On 14 July, Bouterse was re-elected president unopposed; the opposition parties decided that continuity was in the country's best interests. Among the reasons for Bouterse's success was spending on social policies for the improvement of education, housing, healthcare and pensions, but on retaking office, he was forced to introduce severe austerity measures to cope with the collapse in prices for the country's main exports, bauxite and gold. The economy went into reverse in 2015-2016 (GDP contracted by 2.7% in 2015 and an estimated 9% in 2016 – IMF figures), many businesses were forced to close and inflation began to rise. The Recovery and Stabilization Plan 2016-2018 set out reforms which, it was hoped, would arrest the decline through fiscal and monetary policies and stimulation of the private sector, coupled with significant spending on infrastructure and energy projects.

People

Guyana
Population in 2016 was 735,909. Population growth was 0.17%; infant mortality rate 31.5 per 1000 live births; literacy rate 88.5%; GDP per capita US$7500 (2015).

Until the 1920s there was little natural increase in population, but the eradication of malaria and other diseases has since led to rapid expansion, particularly among the East Indians (Asian). The 2002 census showed the following ethnic distribution: East Indian 43.5%; black 30.2%; mixed 16.7%; Amerindian 9.2%; Chinese 0.2%; Portuguese 0.2%; white 0.1%. The latest census was taken in September 2012. Preliminary reports indicated a total population of 747,884, a 0.04% decline since the last census of 2002, but at the time of going to press, detailed analysis of ethnic distribution had not been released. Descendants of the original **Amerindian inhabitants** are divided into nine ethnic groups, including the Akawaio, Arawak, Makushi, Patomona, Wai Wai and Wapishana (full details are on http://indigenouspeoples.gov.gy). Some have lost their isolation and moved to the urban areas, others keenly maintain aspects of their traditional culture and identity. The 2012 census did show that 89.1% of the population lived in the coastal regions, including the capital.

Suriname
Population in 2016 was 585,824. Population growth was 1.05%; infant mortality rate 25.3 per 1000 live births; literacy rate 95.6%; GDP per capita US$16,300 (2015).

The estimated make-up of the population is: **Indo-Pakistanis** (known locally as Hindustanis), 37%; **Creoles** (European-African and other descent), 31%; **Javanese**, 15%; **Maroons** (retribalized descendants of slaves who escaped in the 17th century, living on the upper Saramacca, Suriname and Marowijne rivers), formerly called bush negroes, 10%; **Europeans**, **Chinese** and others, 5%; **Amerindians**, 2%. About 90% of the existing population live in or around Paramaribo or in the coastal towns; the remainder, mostly Carib, Arawak and Maroons, are widely scattered. The main Maroon groups are the Aluku (Boni), Ndjuka (Aucaner), Paramacca, Saramacca, Matawai, and Kwinti (the name Maroon derives from the Spanish *cimarrón* meaning runaway or wild – see http://www.folklife.si.edu/resources/maroon/educational_guide/23.htm for a good introduction). The Asian people originally entered the country as contracted estate labourers, and settled in agriculture or commerce after completion of their term. They dominate the countryside, whereas Paramaribo is racially very mixed. Although some degree of racial tension exists between all the different groups, Creole-Hindustani rivalry is not as fundamental an issue as it is in Guyana, for example. Many Surinamese, of all backgrounds, pride themselves on their ability to get along with each other in such a heterogeneous country.

Guyane
Total population in 2016 was estimated by the UN at 275,688. Population growth in 2016 was estimated at 2.64%, same source (infant mortality rate was 10 per 1000 live births, 2010-2015.

There are widely divergent estimates for the ethnic composition of the population. Calculations vary according to the number included of illegal immigrants, attracted by social benefits and the high living standards. In broad terms, between 30 and 50% of the population are Créoles. Haitians represent about 20% of the total, Europeans 10-14% (of whom about 95% are from France), Brazilians 8%, Asians 4-5% (3-4% from China and Hong Kong, 1-2% from Laos), with about 4% from Suriname and 2.5% from Guyana. The **Amerindian population** is put between 3 and 4%. The main groups are Kali'na/Galibi (Caribs), Arawak (Lokono), Wayana, Palikur, Wayampi-Oyampi and Emerillon/Teka. There are also Maroons, formerly called bush negroes (same groups as in Suriname), who live mostly in the Maroni area, and others (Dominicans, St Lucians, etc) at 0.7%.

Guyana
Land area: 215,083 sq km.

Guyana is nearly the size of Britain, but only about 2.5% is cultivated. About 90% of the population lives on the narrow coastal plain, either in Georgetown, the capital, or in villages along the main road running from Charity in the west to the Suriname border. The rivers give some access to the interior beyond which are the jungles and highlands towards the border with Brazil.

The **coastal plain** is mostly below sea level. Large wooden houses stand on stilts above ground level. A sea wall keeps out the Atlantic and the fertile clay soil is drained by a system of dykes; sluice gates, *kokers*, are opened to let out water at low tide. Separate channels irrigate fields in dry weather. (A similar system operates in Suriname.) Most of the western third of the coastal plain is undrained and uninhabited. Four **major rivers** cross the coastal plain. From west to east they are the Essequibo, the Demerara, the Berbice, and the Corentyne. The Demerara and Berbice are crossed by bridges. Elsewhere ferries must be used. At the mouth of the Essequibo River, 34 km wide, are islands the size of Barbados. The lower reaches of these rivers are navigable; but waterfalls and rapids prevent them being used by large boats to reach the interior. (The area west of the Essequibo River, about 70% of the national territory, is claimed by Venezuela.) The **jungles** and the **highlands** inland from the coastal plain, are thick rainforest, although in the east there is a large area of grassland. Towards Venezuela the rainforest rises in a series of steep escarpments, with spectacular waterfalls, the highest and best known of which are the Kaieteur Falls on the Potaro river. In the southwest is the Rupununi Savannah, an area of grassland as easily reached from Brazil as from Georgetown.

Suriname
Land area: 163,820 sq km. (A large area in the southwest is in dispute with Guyana. There is a less serious border dispute with Guyane in the southeast.)

Like its neighbours, Suriname has a coastline on the Atlantic to the north. The principal rivers are the Marowijne in the east, the Corantijn in the west, and the Suriname, Commewijne (with its tributary, the Cottica), Coppename, Saramacca and Nickerie. The country is divided into topographically quite diverse natural regions: the northern lowlands, 25 km wide in the east and 80 km wide in the west, have clay soil covered with swamps. There follows a region, 5-6 km wide, of a loamy and very white sandy soil, then an undulating region, about 30 km wide. It is mainly savannah, mostly covered with quartz sand, and overgrown with grass and shrubs. South of this lies the interior highland, almost entirely overgrown with dense tropical forest, intersected by streams. At the southern boundary with Brazil there are savannah.

Guyane
Land area: 83,900-86,504 sq km (estimate).

Guyane has its eastern frontier with Brazil formed partly by the river Oiapoque (Oyapock in French) and its southern, also with Brazil, formed by the Tumucumaque mountains (the only range of importance). The western frontier with Suriname is along the river Maroni-Lawa-Litani. To the north is the Atlantic coastline of 320 km. The land rises gradually from a coastal strip some 15-40 km wide to the higher slopes and plains or savannahs, about 80 km inland. Forests cover the hills and valleys of the interior, and the territory is well watered, for over 20 rivers run to the Atlantic.

Music

The Guianas have some of the most interesting and unexpected ethnic mixes in South America: Caribbean and East Indian, Amerindian, Dutch and Javanese, West African, Hmong, French, British and Garifuna. While the music is strongly influenced by the Caribbean, particularly Jamaica (through **reggae** and **dub**) and Trinidad (through **calypso** and **soca**), the music of the three countries reflects this diversity. In Georgetown you'll hear Jamaican reggae alongside Bollywood film music and South Asian Guianese music from the likes of Berbice-born Terry Gajraj (www.terrygajraj.com), whose spicey mix of soca, reggae and Indian singing is known as **chutney** music. And you'll hear **shanto**, Trinidad calypso with a Guyanese spin and mischievous lyrics, and local pop, reggae and soca from a diverse roll call of musicians from established names like Eddy Grant (who had big international hits with *Baby Come Back* and *I Don't Want to Dance*) and newer faces like Fojo. Grant and Fojo live outside Guyana (Barbados and Trinidad respectively), as do other musicians with Guyanese roots, such as UK-based dub producer The Mad Professor and Canadian artist Melanie Fiona.

In Cayenne and Paramaribo there's energetic French Antillean **zouk** which swept out of Guadaloupe and across France in the 1990s, and **kaseko**, one of the most exciting sounds on the continent, a swirling, fast-paced fusion of African and Caribbean music played by the likes of Yakki Famirie, with a called vocal and choral response sung in *papamiento*, Creole or Dutch over frenetic percussion. It is impossible to keep still to. Kaseko was first popularized by Lieve Hugo (also called Iko, Julius Theodoor Hugo Uiterloo, 1934-1975) and as well as percussion includes piano, guitar and brass instruments. Another popular kaseko band is Sabaku. The most traditional form of Surinamese music is **kawina**, which is just singing accompanied by a wide variety of percussion instruments; listen to Sukrusani or Ai Sasie. **Kaskawi** is a blend of kaseko, kawina and other styles and has a strong spiritual element, as does the music played in Javanese communities. The annual Suriname Jazz Festival (http://jazzfestivalsuriname.com) blends local styles with jazz each October. Other styles you may come across in either Suriname or Guyane are **bigi pokoe**, the Maroon-influenced **aléké** and the traditional music and dance of the Maroon culture. Finally there's Caribbean carnival music. Cayenne prides itself on having one of the best Caribbean carnivals outside Trinidad (see Festivals, page 13).

History and travel

Gerald Durrell *Three Singles to Adventure (1954).* Durrell's account of his zoological expedition to British Guiana in 1950.

John Gimlette *The Wild Coast: Travels on South America's Untamed Edge (2011).* Recounting Gimlette's travels in Guyana, Suriname and Guyane, part history, part travelogue.

John Harrison *Off the Map: The Call of the Amazonian Wild.* Republished as *Into the Amazon: An Incredible Story of Survival in the Jungle (2011).* About a canoe expedition across the Tumucumaque Mountains from Brazil to Maripasoula in Guyane. A follow up to *Up the Creek* (1986).

Charles Nicholl *The Creature in the Map: A Journey to El Dorado (1995).* A study of Sir Walter Ralegh and the enduring legend of El Dorado.

Matthew Parker *Willoughbyland: England's Lost Colony (2015).* The story of the founding and collapse of England's first colony in Suriname and its significance in the growth of Empire.

Mark J Plotkin *Tales of a Shaman's Apprentice (1993).* Ethnobotanist Plotkin's report of his search for medicines in the rainforest is set largely in the Guianas.

Charles Waterton *Wanderings in South America (1825, 1878, 1984).* Waterton travelled 3 times to Guyana and Suriname between 1812 and 1820; this book recounts his fascination for the natural history of the region.

Graham Watkins, with photography by Pete Oxford and Renée Bish *Rupununi: Rediscovering a Lost World (2010)*

Evelyn Waugh *Ninety Two Days: A Journey in Guiana and Brazil (1932).* Waugh takes a break from London society in the jungle and savannah of British Guiana; by all accounts he didn't enjoy it very much.

There are many studies of the colonization of the Guianas, the introduction and experience of slavery and, subsequently, of indentured labour and of Maroon culture (on the last, see for example the work of Richard Price: *Maroon Societies: Rebel Slave Communities in the Americas*, edited by Richard Price (1979, 1996) – Part 6 is on Guianas). The legacy of slavery is one of the main features in much contemporary fiction, but not just in the Guianas themselves as Guyanese and Surinamese writers often live outside the country and extend their coverage of the topic to elsewhere in the Americas and the Caribbean (see for example the works of novelist, playwright and poet Fred D'Aguiar, whose 1st novel, *The Longest Memory* (1994) is set in Virginia, while his most recent, *Children of Paradise* (2014) concerns the 1978 Jonestown massacre in Guyana).

Literature

The Oxford Book of Caribbean Short Stories, edited by Stewart Brown and John Wickham (1999), includes writers from Guyana and Suriname and is a good introduction.

Guyana
Wilson Harris *Palace of the Peacock (1960).* The 1st novel in Harris' *Guyana Quartet* concerns a tragic river expedition with a deeply symbolic meaning. Harris has written many

more novels, frequently experimental, and books of non-fiction.

Roy Heath *From the Heat of the Day (1979)*. The 1st of the Armstrong Trilogy of novels about the life of a family in Georgetown, starting in 1922. See also *The Shadow Bride* (1988).

Oonya Kempadoo *Buxton Spice (1998)*. Kempadoo's 1st novel is about a teenager growing up in a village on the Guyanese coast in the 1970s. She has subsequently written *Tide Running* (2001) and *All Decent Animals* (2013).

Pauline Melville *The Ventriloquist's Tale (1997)*. A novel by writer and actress Melville about a mixed Scottish/Amerindian family in 20th-century Guyana. Her other works include *Shapeshifter* (1990) and *The Migration of Ghosts* (1998).

Suriname

Very few Surinamese writers have been translated into English. Among acclaimed writers are Albert Helman, 1903-96 (*Zuid-zuid west* – 1926, and *De stille plantage* – *The Silent Plantation*, 1931), the prolific poet and novelist, Astrid Roemer, 1947 –, and Clark Accord (1961-2011), whose *De koningin van Paramaribo* (*The Queen of Paramaribo*, 1999) about a prostitute, Wilhelmina Rijburg, in Paramaribo, was a bestseller. Karin Amatmoekrim's (b1977) novel *De man an veel* (*The Man of Many*, 2013) is about Anton de Kom, a Surinamese anti-colonialist who eventually died in a Nazi concentration camp. Tessa Leuwsha (b1967) published *Fansi's stilte* (2015) following the life of her Surinamese grandmother back to the days of slavery. The best-known Surinamese writer whose work is available in English is Cynthia McLeod (b1936), whose *The Cost of Sugar* (*Hoe duur was de suiker*, 1987) about early Jewish settlers and the tragic relationship between half-sisters, was made into a film in 2013. *The Free Negress Elisabeth* (*De vrije negerin Elisabeth*, 2000), about the richest woman in Suriname in the 18th century, Elisabeth Samson, is also translated into English.

Guyane

Without a doubt, the most famous book about Guyane is Henri Charrière's *Papillon* (1969), about his imprisonment and escape from the penal colony. Although the authenticity of the story has been questioned by some, the book has never lost its popularity, which was certainly boosted by the 1973 film of it starring Steve McQueen and Dustin Hoffman.

Léon-Gontran Damas (1912-1978), born in Cayenne, educated in Martinique and Paris, was possibly one of the most influential black writers of the 20th century for his part in the founding of the Négritude movement in the 1930s together with Aimé Césaire and Léopold Sédar Senghor. Among the movement's ideals was a common racial identity for black people worldwide.

Practicalities

Getting there

Air

Guyana

There are international flights to Guyana from the US, the Caribbean, Brazil and Suriname. **Caribbean Airlines** ⓘ *91-92 Av of the Republic and Regent St, T1-800-744 2225, or 261 2202, www.caribbean-airlines.com*, flies to Port of Spain, Trinidad, with connections throughout the Caribbean and to Miami, and direct to New York and Toronto, plus to London (in a codeshare with **BA**). **Surinam Airways** ⓘ *110 Duke and Barrack St, Kingston, T225 4249, www.flyslm.com*, flies Suriname–Guyana–Miami three times a week. **TGA** ⓘ *Ogle, T222 2525, http://transguyana.net*, in a codeshare with **GUM Air** (see below) flies Georgetown–Paramaribo daily (two a day Monday-Friday, once a day Saturday and Sunday). Other carriers include **Eastern Airlines/ Guyana One** ⓘ *http://easternairlines.aero, or www.travelspan.com*, flying between Guyana and New York and Miami; **Dynamic** ⓘ *https://airdynamic.com*, flying between New York and Georgetown; **Fly Jamaica** ⓘ *www.fly-jamaica.com*, flying between Guyana and Jamaica; and **Copa** ⓘ *www.copaair.com*, from Panama to Georgetown four days a week.

Suriname

The following airlines have international flights to Suriname: **Surinam Airways** ⓘ *Dr Sophie Redmondstraat 219, T432700, www.flyslm.com*, to/from Amsterdam, joint operation with **KLM** ⓘ *Burenstraat 33, T411811 ext 3*; Miami via Aruba and via Georgetown twice a week; Belém via Cayenne (see below); Port of Spain and Curaçao. **Caribbean Airlines** ⓘ *Wagenwegstraat 36, T520034, www. caribbean-airlines.com*, to/from Port of Spain. **Gum Air** ⓘ *Doekhieweg 03, Zorg en Hoop Airport, T498760, info@gumair.com*, with **Trans Guyana** ⓘ *T433830*, fly Paramaribo–Georgetown daily. **Fly Allways** ⓘ *Aidastraat 9, Paramaribo, T455645, http://flyallways.com, and 42 Croal St and United Nations, Georgetown, T226 8359*, fly between Paramaribo and Georgetown and Barbados. For **Air France** (flights between Cayenne and Europe), as for **KLM**, above.

Guyane

For international flights to France and the French Caribbean islands contact **Air Caraïbes** ⓘ *Félix Éboué airport, T308450, www.aircaraibes.com*, which flies to Paris; also **Air France** ⓘ *T298785, www.airfrance.com*. **Surinam Airways** ⓘ *15 rue Louis Blanc, T293000, www.flyslm.com*, flies to Paramaribo Monday, Wednesday, Thursday, Saturday, and to Belém. Brazilian airline **Azul** ⓘ *www.voeazul.com.br*, also flies to Belém.

TRAVEL TIP
Driving in the Guianas

Guyana
Roads Most coastal towns are linked by a good 296-km road from Springlands in the east to Charity in the west; the Essequibo river is crossed by ferry, the Berbice by a toll bridge and the Demerara by a toll bridge, which, besides closing at high tide for ships to pass through (two to three hours) is subject to frequent closures. Apart from a good road connecting Timehri and Linden, continuing as dirt to Mabura Hill and then on to Lethem on the border with Brazil, most other roads in the interior are very poor.

Safety Traffic drives on the left.

Documents No *carnet de passages* is required for driving a private vehicle. If you are bringing a private car into Guyana, policy differs over how many days you are given. You may be given 30 days at Springlands, but only three at Lethem.

Car hire Several companies in Georgetown (most are listed in the Yellow Pages of the phone directory). A permit is needed from local police; it can be applied for at Cheddi Jagan International Airport or at the Guyana Revenue Authority office, 200-201 Camp St, Georgetown. Rental agencies can advise.

Fuel Gasoline (Mogas) costs US$0.91 a litre; diesel US$0.79.

Suriname
Roads 26% of roads are paved. East–west roads: From Albina to Paramaribo to Nieuw–Nickerie is paved. North-south roads: the road Paramaribo–Paranam–Afobakka–Pokigron is open. The road to the western interior, Zanderij–Apura, crosses the Coppename River; thereafter small bridges are in poor shape (take planks to bridge gaps). On the unpaved Moengo–Blakawatra road (eastern Suriname), the bridge across the Commewijne River is closed to traffic.

Road

Guyana
Minibuses and collective taxis run between the ferry from Suriname and Georgetown and minibuses run daily from Lethem on the border with Brazil to Georgetown.

Suriname
Public transport (minibuses and shared taxis) runs from both the border with Guyana and the border with Guyane to Paramaribo.

Guyane
The main coastal road from St-Laurent du Maroni on the Suriname border to Cayenne and on to Saint-Georges-de-l'Oyapock on the Brazil border is about 450 km of paved road. It is possible to travel overland to Cayenne from Suriname and onwards to Macapá in Brazil. The latter takes about 24 hours from Cayenne

Note The Surinaamse Auto Rally Klub, www.sarkonline.com, has information on rallying and other motoring events.

Road safety Driving is on the left, but some vehicles have left-hand drive. There is a 24-hour emergency service for motorists: Wegenwacht, Sr Winston Churchillweg 123, T484691/487540.

Documents All driving licences accepted; you need a stamp from the local police and a deposit. To drive a foreign-registered vehicle requires no carnet or other papers. You must have two years on your driving licence. A surcharge is made on drivers under 21. People wishing to travel from Suriname to either Guyana or Guiane by car need special vehicle insurance, available from **Assuria Insurance Company**, Grote Combeweg 37, Paramaribo, T473400, www. assuria.sr. Although an international driver's licence is accepted in Suriname and Guyana, a special permit is required to drive for longer than one month.

Car hire There are several car rental companies in Paramaribo (see page 74). Rates start at about US$40 for 1-2 days for the smallest car (US$210 for a week), rising to US$92 (US$500 per week) for a pick-up.

Fuel Gasoline is sold as diesel, 'regular', unleaded, or super unleaded (more expensive): US$0.65-0.70 per litre.

Guyane

Roads The main road, narrow, but paved, runs for 270 km from Pointe Macouris, on the roadstead of Cayenne, to Mana and St-Laurent. It also runs to Régina and St-Georges de l'Oyapock on the Brazilian border.

Safety Traffic drives on the right.

Documents There are no formalities for bringing a private car across the Guyane–Suriname border, but you must ensure that your insurance is valid.

Car hire The most popular way to get around.

Fuel Gasoline/petrol costs about €1.50/US$1.65 per litre. Diesel/gazole €1.27/US$1.40 per litre.

with half a day's waiting in St-Georges de l'Oyapock for the Brazilian bus to leave. The roads are generally good. Combis (minivans) ply the roads between St-Laurent, Cayenne and St-Georges.

Getting around

Air

Guyana

Most flights to the interior leave from Ogle, some 15 minutes from Georgetown. For scheduled flights between Georgetown and Lethem see page 56, and services to Kaieteur and Rupununi, see page 54. Scheduled services to many parts of Guyana and charters are offered by **Trans Guyana Airways (TGA)** ⓘ *Ogle, T222 2525, http://transguyana.net*; **Air Services Limited (ASL)** ⓘ *Ogle, T222 1234, www.aslgy.com*; **Sky West Travel** ⓘ *Ogle, T225 4206, Facebook:skywestcharter* *(to northwestern Guyana)*, and **Air Guyana–Wings** ① *Ogle, T222 6513, www.airguyana.biz*. **Roraima Airways** ① *RAL, Lot 8 Eping Av, Bel Air Park, Georgetown, T225 9647, www.roraimaairways.com*, and **Golden Arrow Airways** ① *64 C Middle St, Georgetown, T226 0378, reservations@goldenarrowairways.com*, operate only charter flights out of **Ogle**. Domestic airlines are very strict on baggage allowance on internal flights: 20 lb per person.

Suriname
Internal services are run by **Gum Air** (address above), a small air charter firm. **Hi Jet** is a helicopter charter company at **Zorg en Hoop airport** ① *T432577*. There are no scheduled flights, only charters. The air companies fly to several Amerindian and Maroon villages. Most settlements have an airstrip, but internal air services are limited. These flights are on demand.

Guyane
Air Guyane ① *Félix Éboué airport, T293630, www.airguyane.com*, handles all domestic flights. Schedules are given in the text above.

River

Guyana
There are over 960 km of navigable river, an important means of communication. In addition to the ferries and river boats described here also contact the Transport and Harbours Department, Water St, Georgetown. Six-seater river boats are called *ballahoos*, three- to four-seaters are *corials*; they provide the transport in the forest. The ferry across the Corentyne to Suriname carries vehicles; it operates once or twice daily.

Suriname
As in Guyana, rivers are an important and, in many cases, the only means of communication in Suriname. The length of navigable rivers is roughly the same as in its neighbour. Cruises can be taken on the Suriname and Commewijne rivers near Paramaribo and some agencies make long-distance expeditions by boat. Where the road network ends, south of the Brokopondo reservoir, river boat is the only mode of transport, other than to the few places with an airstrip.

Guyane
The Maroni river (border with Suriname) has frequent boat services upriver from St-Laurent. There is a more limited river service on the Oyapock (border with Brazil). The other places where boat trips can be taken are Roura and Kaw.

Road

Guyana

Minibuses and collective taxis run between Georgetown and the entire coast from Charity to Corriverton; also to Linden. Minibuses run daily from Georgetown to Lethem. All taxis have an H on the number plate and it is recommended that you only use those painted yellow.

Suriname

Details of buses and taxis are given in the text in Transport sections. Hitchhiking is possible but neither common nor advisable.

Guyane

See the Guyane chapter for transport from the borders with Suriname and Brazil to Cayenne. The bus and shared taxi terminal in the capital is the Gare routière at corner of rue Molé and Avenue de la Liberté beside the Canal Laussat. Transport is expensive. Hitchhiking is reported to be easy and widespread.

Maps

There is a recommended *ITMB* (International Travel Maps and Books) map that includes Guyana, Suriname and Guyane; they also publish a separate map on "Surinam and French Guiana".

Guyana

Maps of country and Georgetown (US$20) from **Department of Lands and Surveys** ⓘ *Homestreet Av, Durban Backland (take a taxi), T226 0524 in advance*, poor stock. Rivers and islands change frequently, so maps only give a general direction. A local guide can be more reliable. Free country and city maps are available from most tour operators and hotels. Georgetown and Guyana maps can be found in *Explore Guyana magazine*.

Suriname

Some maps can be found in **Readytex** ⓘ *Maagdenstraat 44-48, behind Hotel Krasnapolsky, www.readytexartgallery.com, Mon-Fri 0800-1630, Sat 0830-1330*, and at **Vaco bookshop** ⓘ *Domineestraat 26, T472545*.

Guyane

The **IGN** publishes a 1:400,000 country map with details of towns and a series of maps covering the coast at 1:25,000. Another map is available at www.map-france.com or www.cartesfrance.fr. The **Comité du Tourisme de la Guyane** also has a tourist map.

Essentials A-Z

Accident and emergency

Guyana
Police: T911 (24-hr emergency response T225 6411); **Fire**: T912; **Ambulance**: T913.

Suriname
Police: Emergency T115; other police numbers in Paramaribo T471111/7777, www.politie.sr. **Medical emergency**: T113. **Fire Brigade**: T110.

Guyane
General emergency number: T112; also **police**: T17, **medical emergency**: T15, **fire**: T18.

Electricity

Guyana
220-240 volts, but 110 volts in Georgetown; 60 cycles. In lodges with their own generators, ask if unsure of the voltage. Plugs as in US: 2 flat pin, or 2 flat pin and a half-round earth pin. You may also find 3 round pin and 3 flat pin, UK-style plugs.

Suriname
110/127 volts AC, 60 cycles. Plug fittings: usually 2-pin round (European continental type).

Guyane
220 volts, 50 cycles. Plugs are the same as mainland Europe.

Embassies and consulates

Guyana
For a full list of Guyanese overseas representatives and of foreign representation in Guyana, visit http://embassy.goabroad.com.

Suriname
For all Surinamese embassies and consulates abroad and for all foreign embassies and consulates in Suriname, see http://embassy.goabroad.com.

Guyane
A full list of France's overseas representation can be found at www.mfe.org or http://embassy.goabroad.com.

Health

See your GP or travel clinic at least 6 weeks before departure for general advice on travel risks and vaccinations. Try phoning a specialist travel clinic if your own doctor is unfamiliar with health in the region. Make sure you have sufficient medical travel insurance, get a dental check, know your own blood group and, if you suffer a long-term condition such as diabetes or epilepsy, obtain a Medic Alert bracelet (www.medicalert.org.uk).

Vaccinations and anti-malarials
Confirm that your primary courses and boosters are up to date. It is advisable to vaccinate against polio, tetanus, typhoid, hepatitis A and, for more remote areas, rabies. Yellow fever vaccination is obligatory for most areas. Cholera, diphtheria and hepatitis B vaccinations are sometimes advised. Specialist advice should be taken on the best antimalarials to take before you leave.

Health risks

The major risks posed in the region are those caused by insect disease carriers such as mosquitoes and sandflies. The key parasitic and viral diseases are malaria, South American trypanosomiasis (Chagas' disease) and dengue fever. Be aware that you are always at risk from these diseases. **Malaria** is a danger throughout the lowland tropics and coastal regions. **Dengue fever**, which is widespread, is particularly hard to protect against as the mosquitoes can bite throughout the day as well as night (unlike those that carry malaria). In 2015 cases of the chikungunya virus, transmitted by the same mosquito that carries dengue, had been confirmed in all South American countries except Argentina, Chile and Uruguay. Cases of the **Zika virus**, similarly spread, have been reported in many countries throughout the region in 2015 and 2016. Try to wear clothes that cover arms and legs and also use effective mosquito repellent. Mosquito nets dipped in permethrin provide a good physical and chemical barrier at night. **Chagas' disease** is spread by faeces of the triatomine, or assassin bugs, whereas sandflies spread a disease of the skin called **leishmaniasis**. Some form of diarrhoea or intestinal upset is almost inevitable, the standard advice is always to wash your hands before eating and to be careful with drinking water and ice; if you have any doubts about the water then boil it or filter and treat it. In a restaurant buy bottled water or ask where the water has come from. Food can also pose a problem, be wary of salads if you don't know whether they have been washed or not.

If you get sick

Contact your embassy or consulate for a list of doctors and dentists who speak your language, or at least some English. Your hotel may also be able to recommend good local medical services.

Medical services

For hospitals, doctors and dentists, ask at your hotel or else contact your consulate or the tourist office for advice.

Guyana

Well-equipped private hospitals in Georgetown include: **Balwant Singh**, 314 East St, South Cummingsburg, T225 4279/227 1087, http://drbalwantsinghshospital.com; **Prashad's**, Middle St and Thomas St, doctor on call at weekends, 24-hr malaria clinic, T226 7214/9 (US$2 to US$8 per day; medical consultations US$8 to US$15); **St Joseph Mercy**, 130-132 Parade St, Kingston, T227 2073/5. If admitted to hospital you must bring sheets and food (St Joseph's provides these). **Georgetown Hospital** is understaffed even though facilities have improved.

Suriname

Academic Hospital (Academisch Ziekenhuis), Flustraat, Paramaribo, T442222, www.azp.sr. **Sint Vincentius Ziekenhuis**, Koninginnestraat 4, Paramaribo, T471212, www.svzsuriname.org.

Guyane

Centre Hospitalier Andrée Rosemond, Av des Flamboyants, 97300 Cayenne, T395050, www.ch-cayenne.net. Health information and list of other clinics can be found on www.guyane-amazonie.fr/infos-pratiques.

Language

In **Guyana** English is the common language. In **Suriname**, the official language is Dutch. Sranan Tongo, originally the speech of the Créoles, is now the lingua franca understood by all groups. English is widely used. In **Guyane** French is the main language, but in Cayenne you will find some English, Spanish and Portuguese spoken. Créole is also commonly used. Officials do not usually (or deliberately) speak anything other than French.

In all 3 countries, the Asians, Maroons and Amerindians speak their own languages among themselves.

Money

Guyana

US$1 = G$203; €1 = G$216 (Apr 2017).

Exchange The unit is the Guyanese dollar. There are notes for 20, 50, 100, 500, 1000 and 5000 dollars. Coins are for 1, 5 and 10 dollars. Official exchange rate is adjusted weekly in line with the rate offered by licensed exchange houses (*cambios*). There are ATMs in Georgetown. Also take cash dollars or euros. They only buy US or Canadian dollars, euros and pounds sterling. Most *cambios* accept drafts (subject to verification) and telegraphic transfers, but not credit cards. Rates vary slightly between *cambios* and from day to day and some *cambios* offer better rates for changing over US$100. **Republic Bank** and *cambios* accept euros at best rates. A reputable, safe *cambio* in Georgetown is **Hand in Hand Trust Corporation**, Middle St, T226 9781, next to **Rima Guest House**. Take care with the roving *cambios* at the entrance to Stabroek market. To buy Suriname dollars, go to **Swiss House**, 25a Water St, a *cambio* in the unsafe market area around Water St and America St, known locally as 'Wall St'. There are others that will change Suriname dollars. Note that to sell Guyanese dollars on leaving, you will need to produce your *cambio* receipt. The black market on America St in Georgetown still operates, but rates offered are no better than the *cambio* rate. To avoid being robbed on the black market, or if you need to change money when *cambios* are closed, go by taxi and ask someone (preferably a friend) to negotiate for you. The black market also operates in Molson Creek/Springlands, the entry point from Suriname, and in Lethem at the Brazilian border (ask taxi drivers).

Cost of travelling Devaluation means that, for foreigners, prices for food and drink are low at present. Even imported goods may be cheaper than elsewhere and locally produced goods such as fruit are very cheap. Hotels, tours and services in the interior are subject to energy and fuel surcharges, making them less cheap.

Suriname

US$1 = SRD7.55, €1 = SRD8.04 (Apr 2017).

Exchange The unit of currency is the Suriname dollar (SRD), divided into 100 cents. There are notes for 1, 2.50, 5, 10, 20, 50 and 100 dollars. Coins are for 1 and 2.50 dollars and 1, 5, 10 and 25 cents (the 25-cent coin is usually known as a *kwartje*, 10-cent *dubbeltje* and 5-cent *stuiver*). Euros are readily exchanged in banks and with licensed money changers (*cambios*). The main banks that offer exchange are: **de Surinaamsche Bank**; **Finabank** (www.finabanknv.com, open on Sat 0900-1200); **Hakrinbank** (www.hakrinbank.com); **Republic Bank** (www.republicbanksr.com). There are ATMs throughout the city. On arrival at the Johan Adolf Pengel airport, you can exchange a wide variety of currencies into Surinamese dollars, including reais, Trinidad and Tobago dollars and Barbados dollars. In Paramaribo *cambios* at various locations are open till late and on Sat, but only accept US dollars and euros. A good, helpful one is **Multi Track Exchange**, van Sommelsdijkstraat at corner of Kleine Waterstraat, near the Torarica. Officially visitors must declare foreign currency on arrival. When arriving by land, visitors' funds are rarely checked, but you should be prepared for it. To check daily exchange rates for US dollars, euros, pounds sterling and other currencies, visit the **Central Bank** site, www.cbvs.sr. Prices can be quoted in SRD, US dollars or euros; check carefully as there seems to be no logic to it.

Guyane

US$1 = €0.94 (Apr 2017).

Exchange The currency is the euro. Take euros with you; many banks do not offer exchange facilities, but ATMs are common. Good rates can be obtained by using Visa or MasterCard (less common) to withdraw cash from any bank in Cayenne, Kourou and St-Laurent du Maroni. It is possible to pay for most hotels and restaurants with a Visa or MasterCard. American Express, Eurocard and Carte Bleue cards are also accepted. Most banks have ATMs for cash withdrawals on Visa and MasterCard. There's an exchange facility at the airport. A convenient cambio is **Global – Changes Caraïbes**, 68 av Général de Gaulle, Cayenne, open Mon-Fri 0730-1200, 1500-1730, changes US$ and reais into euros. Central pharmacy may help when banks are closed. It's almost impossible to change dollars outside Cayenne or Kourou.

Opening hours

Guyana
Banks: Mon-Thu 0800-1400, Fri 0800-1430. **Markets**: Mon-Sat 0800-1600, except Wed 0900-1200, Sun 0800-1000. **Shops**: Mon-Fri 0830-1600 or 1700, Sat 0830-1200.

Suriname
Banks: Mon-Fri 0900-1400 (airport bank is open when flights operate). **Government offices**: Mon-Thu 0700-1500, Fri 0700-1430. **Shops and businesses**: Mon-Fri 0800-1630 (some shops till 1900 on Fri), Sat 0800-1300. Asian supermarkets tend to keep longer hours.

Guyane
Hours vary widely between different offices, shops and even between different branches of the same bank. There seem to be different business hours for every day, but they are usually posted. Most shops and offices close for a few hours around midday.

Post

Guyana
The main post office is on Robb St, Georgetown, http://guypost.gy. There is another on Regent St, opposite Bourda market. There are postal centres in Lethem and at Rock View, Annai. Post offices are open Mon-Fri 0700-1500, some close 1130-1230; some open Sat 0700-1100.

Suriname
Surpost, Kerkplein 1, Paramaribo, T477 524, www.surpost.com.

Guyane
The main post office is on Route de Baduel, 2 km from the centre of Cayenne (take a taxi or 20 mins on foot).

Public holidays and festivals

Hindu and Muslim festivals

Hindu and Muslim festivals follow a lunar calendar, and dates should be checked as required: **Phagwah**, or **Holi**, usually in **Mar,** date varies each year, is the Hindu spring festival, when everyone is a target for coloured powder and coloured water; **Diwali**, or **Deepavali**, celebrated in the northern hemisphere autumn, is the Hindu Festival of Light, representing the triumph of knowledge, light and goodness over the darkness of ignorance and evil.

Significant dates in the Muslim calendar that are public holidays are **Eid al-Fitr**, end of Ramadan, the 1st day of the month of Shawwal (10th month of the lunar calendar); **Eid al-Adha** is the Feast of Sacrifice on the 10th day of the month of Dhu al-Hijjah, celebrating Ibrahim's (Abraham's) willingness to sacrifice his son; **Youman Nabi**, or **Mawlid al-Nabi**, commemorates the birthday of the Prophet Muhammad on the 12th day of the month of Rabi al-Awwal.

Guyana

1 Jan New Year's Day.
23 Feb Republic Day and Mashramani festival.
Mar (usually) Phagwah.
Mar/Apr Good Fri, Easter Sun and Mon.
1 May Labour Day.
5 May Indian Arrival Day.
26 May Independence Day.
1st Mon Jul Caricom Day.
1st Mon Aug Emancipation Day.
Late Oct-early Nov Diwali (Deepavali). See above.
25-26 Dec Christmas Day and Boxing Day.

Suriname

1 Jan New Year's Day.
25 Feb Day of Liberation and Innovation.
Mar (usually) Phagwah (see above).
Mar/Apr Good Fri, Easter Sun and Mon.
1 May Labour Day.
1 Jul Emancipation Day.
9 Aug Indigenous People's Day, Javanese Immigration Day.
10 Oct Day of the Maroons.
Late Oct-early Nov Diwali (Deepavali).
25 Nov Independence Day.
25-26 Dec Christmas Day and Boxing Day.

Guyane

Public holidays are mostly the same as in Metropolitan France:
1 Jan New Year's Day.
Feb/Mar Carnival.
Mar/Apr Good Fri, Easter Sun and Mon.
1 May Labour Day.
8 May Victory in Europe Day.
25 May Ascension Day.
4-5 Jun Whitsun.
10 Jun Abolition of Slavery Day.
14 Jul Bastille Day.
15 Aug Assumption of Mary.
1 Nov All Saints' Day.
11 Nov Armistice Day.
25-26 Dec Christmas Day and Boxing Day.

Tax

Guyana

Airport tax This is G$6000 (US$30, €28.60), payable in Guyanese dollars or foreign currency equivalent at Cheddi Jagan International airport. This is made up of a G$2500 security fee and a G$3500 departure tax. For international departures from Ogle airport, tax is G$3500 (US$17.70, €16.75). It was announced in Jan 2017 that departure tax will be included in flight tickets. **VAT** 16%.

Suriname
Airport tax Departure tax is included in the air fare.

Guyane
Airport tax None.

Telephone and internet

In all 3 countries internet outside the cities, if available at all, is usually provided by satellite and use is restricted. See Where to stay, Rupununi Savannah (page 43), on internet usage in lodges in Guyana. It is best to not to rely on email or even on mobile reception when in the interior. In the capital cities Wi-Fi can be found in many places and mobile reception is widespread.

Guyana *Country code +592.*
Ringing: a double ring, repeated regularly. **Engaged**: equal tones, separated by equal pauses. Mobile phone reception outside Georgetown is patchy. In the Rupununi, for instance, few lodges have reception although at Annai there is GT&T reception and at Lethem GT&T and Digicel.

Suriname *Country code +597.*
Ringing: equal tones and long pauses. **Engaged**: equal tones with equal pauses. **Telesur**, Heiligenweg 14, Paramaribo, T474242, www.sr.net, with branches nationwide. All **Telesur Dienstencentrum** offices offer email, fax, local and international phone and computer services. Phone cards for cheap international calls are available in newsagents, shops and hotels in

Paramaribo, a better deal than Telesur card. In Nieuw Nickerie the telephone office is with the post office on Oost-Kanaalstraat, between Gouverneurstraat and R P Bharosstraat. If phoning within the city, omit 0 from the prefix. Mobile services are provided by **Telesur** and **Digicel**.

Guyane *Country code +594.*
Ringing: equal tones with long pauses. **Engaged**: equal tones with equal pauses. Mobile services are operated by **Digicel** and **Orange**.

Time

Guyana
GMT -4 hrs; 1 hr ahead of EST (but the same as EST during US daylight saving).

Suriname
GMT -3 hrs.

Guyane
GMT -3 hrs.

Tourist information

Guyana
Guyana Tourism Authority, National Exhibition Center, Sophia, Georgetown, T219 0094, www.guyana-tourism.com, promotes the development of the tourism industry.
Ministry of Business, 229 South Rd, Lacytown, Georgetown, T226 2505, http://minbusiness.gov.gy/tourism/ creates tourism policy.
Tourism and Hospitality Association of Guyana (THAG), 157 Waterloo St, T225 0807, www.exploreguyana.org, is a private organization covering all areas of tourism, with an 80-page, full-colour magazine called *Explore Guyana*, available from the Association office.

Useful websites:
www.guyana.org For information and lots of useful links.
www.guyanabirding.com For birdwatching; see its associated newsletter, *Guyana Birding News*.
www.wwfguianas.org WWF Guianas Programme, the conservation initiative covering the 3 Guianas; offices in Georgetown, 285 Irving St, Queenstown, T223 7802; Paramaribo, Henck Arronstraat 63, Suite E, Paramaribo, T422357; and Cayenne, Lotissement Katoury No 5, Route Montabo 97300, T313828.

Suriname

Suriname Hospitality and Tourism Association SHATA, Kristalstraat 1, Paramaribo, T710 0823, www.shata.sr, is a private organization including hotels and **Surinam Airways**, combining all the private organizations that used to exist independently.

Suriname Tourism Foundation, Dr J F Nassylaan 2, T424878, www.suriname tourism.sr (in English). It publishes *The Official Tourist Destination Guide*.

Useful websites:
http://suriname.conservation. org Conservation International site with information on Suriname including the **Central Suriname Nature Reserve**.
www.whsrn.org Western Hemisphere Shore-bird Reserve Network, in which are the Bigi Pan, Wia Wia and Coppenamemonding reserves.

Guyane

The French Government tourist offices can usually provide leaflets on Guyane; also **Comité du Tourisme de la Guyane**, 1 rue Clapeyron, 75008 Paris, T33-1-4294 1516, bureauparisien@guyane-amazonie.fr, Mon-Fri 0900-1600.

Comité du Tourisme de la Guyane, 12 rue Lallouette, BP 801, 97300 Cayenne, T05-94-296500, www. tourisme-guyane.com. See also www. ctguyane.fr. **Note** The Amerindian villages in the Haut-Maroni and Haut-Oyapock areas may only be visited with permission from the Préfecture in Cayenne *before* arrival in Guyane.

Protected areas:
www.guyane.developpement-durable.gouv.fr has information on the **DEAL Guyane (Direction de l'Environment, de l'Aménagement et du Logement)** with an *Atlas des Sites et Espaces protégés de Guyane* to download. Further information can be found on the French government site **www.reserves-naturelles.org** which has information on all Guyane's national parks. Contact also **PNR de Guyane**, 31 rue François Arago, Cayenne, T289270, www.guyane-parcregional.fr, for Kaw-Roura and Amana, and **www.parc-amazonien-guyane.fr**, which deals specifically with the Parc Amazonien de Guyane.

Visas and immigration

Guyana
The following countries do not need a visa to visit Guyana: Australia, Argentina, Brazil, Canada, Colombia, Ecuador, Japan, New Zealand, Norway, Peru, Switzerland, Uruguay, USA, EU countries (except Cyprus, Czech Republic, Estonia, Hungary, Latvia, Lithuania, Malta, Poland, Slovak Republic and Slovenia) and the Commonwealth countries. Visitors are advised to check with the nearest embassy, consulate or travel agent for changes to this list. All visitors require a passport with 6 months' validity and all nationalities, apart from those above, require visas.

To obtain a visa you will need 2 photos, a letter of sponsorship and sponsor's contact number or email address, evidence of sufficient funds and, if coming from a country with yellow fever, a yellow fever certificate. Visa application forms can be found at **www.minfor. gov.gy** on the consular services pages. If Guyana has no representation in your country, apply to the Guyana Embassy in Washington DC, or the Guyana Consulate General in New York. Tourist visas cost US$25 for a period of 1 month initially, then US$25 for each additional month. Employment and student visas cost US$140 for 3 years in the first instance and an additional US$140 for each 3-year renewal. Business visas cost US$140 for 5 years in the first instance and US$140 for each 5-year renewal. Visitors from those countries where they are required arriving without visas are refused entry, unless a tour operator has obtained permission for the visitor to get a visa on arrival. To fly into Guyana, an exit ticket is required; at land borders an onward ticket is not usually asked for.

Suriname

Visitors must have a valid passport. Nationalities that do not need a visa or tourist card include: Israel, Japan, Malaysia, Philippines, South Korea, Gambia, Argentina, Brazil, Chile, Belize, Guyana and other Caricom member states. Nationals of the following countries may apply for a tourist card: the majority of EU countries (not Bulgaria, Cyprus, Ireland, Poland, Romania), Canada, Cuba, Indonesia, Mexico, Norway, Singapore, Switzerland, Turkey, USA, South American countries (except Argentina and Brazil – see above), Central American countries and foreigners of Surinamese origin. The card is valid for one entry by air of 90 days

(but after 30 days you must apply to the Immigration Department, address below, for an extension); it costs €30/US$35 (exact cash only) and can be obtained at a Surinamese embassy or consulate, the tourist card counter at **Schiphol Airport**, Amsterdam, T020-622 6717 (closed Sunday), or on arrival at Johan Adolf Pengel Airport (there may be long queues here). You need a passport valid for 6 months and a return flight ticket. See under St-Laurent du Maroni, Border with Suriname, page 80, for details of the consulate in Cayenne. If your flights into and out of South America land at and depart from Johan Adolf Pengel Airport and you intend to visit countries in addition to Suriname, you must check whether you need to get a new tourist card to re-enter Suriname for your flight home.

For all other nationals, to obtain a visa in advance, you must apply to a Surinamese embassy or consulate up to 6 weeks before your scheduled departure to Suriname. You need to fill in an application form (which can be obtained online on consular websites) and submit it with a copy of your passport photo page, valid for 6 months, and a computer-generated itinerary or round-trip ticket. You will then be issued with a letter and another form to be completed with a passport photo and presented on arrival at Johan Pengel Airport where the visa fee must be paid. A 3-month tourist visa, single entry: €40; multiple entry: €40/US$42 for 3 months, €150 (US$158) for 12 months. A visa for US passport holders is US$100 for 5 years, multiple entry. A transit visa costs €10 (US$10.55). A business visa costs from €50 (US$53) (2 months) to €300 (US$316 – 2 years). See the websites of the Suriname consulate in The Netherlands, www.

consulaatsuriname.nl, the embassy in the US, www.surinameembassy.org, or consulate in Miami, surcgmia@bellsouth.net, for latest details (prices vary in some cases). If arriving by land or sea, you cannot use a Visa on Arrival document; you must obtain a visa sticker from a consulate. Procedures at consulates vary: in Cayenne visa applications normally take 1 day, 2 passport photos are required. In Georgetown visa applications can be submitted at any time, but only collected when the consular section is open on Mon, Wed and Fri morning. If applying when the consulate is open, visas are usually processed on the same day. Make sure your name on the visa matches exactly that on your passport. On entry into Suriname (by land or air) your passport will be stamped by immigration for 30 days. If you wish to stay in Suriname longer than 3 months, you must apply within 2 weeks of arrival in Suriname (at least 3 months if you are visa holder) for **Authorization of Temporary Stay** (Machtiging Kort Verblijf, MVK) which is subject to a €10 administration fee, a €40 or US$42 fee and a US$150 finalization charge. MVK applications must be sent to a Suriname consulate or embassy. An exit stamp is given by the Immigration office at the airport or land border. If you want a multiple-entry visa or have any other enquiries, go to the **Immigration Department/Registration of Foreigners**, Mr J Lachmonstraat 166-8, Paramaribo, T597-490666, Mon-Fri 0700-1430, or **the Ministry of Foreign Affairs**, consular section, Lim A Po Straat and Watermolen straat, Paramaribo, T473575, sec.conza@foreignaffairs.gov.sr.

Note If you are arriving from Guyana, Guyane or Brazil in theory you need a certificate of vaccination against yellow fever to be allowed entry. It is not always asked for.

Guyane

Passports are not required by nationals of France and most French-speaking African countries carrying identity cards. For EU visitors, documents are the same as for Metropolitan France (that is no visa, no exit ticket required – check with a consulate in advance). EU passports must be stamped if arriving overland from Suriname or Brazil; be sure to visit Immigration, it is easy to miss. If arriving by air, EU citizens are not required to get an entry stamp, although you can join the queue for non-EU citizens to get one, or at least ask if you should have one. There is nowhere in Cayenne to get an entry stamp, only at the airport.
Note Whether or not you have an entry stamp, you must get an exit stamp. No visa required for most nationalities (except for those of Guyana, Suriname, some Eastern European countries – not Croatia – and Asian – not Japan – and other African countries) for a stay of up to 3 months. A flight ticket out of the country is required in theory (a ticket out of one of the other Guianas is also in theory not sufficient); a deposit is required otherwise. It is not always asked for, especially for EU citizens. Likewise, a yellow fever vaccination certificate is also required if arriving from Brazil, Suriname or Guyana, but it is not always asked for. If you stay more than 3 months, income tax clearance is required before leaving the country. A visa costs €60, or equivalent (US$63).

Weights and measures

All 3 countries are officially metric, although imperial is still widely used in Guyana.

Index

*Entries in **bold** refer to maps*

Advertisers' index

About the author

One of the first assignments **Ben Box** took as a freelance writer in 1980 was subediting work on the *South American Handbook*. The plan then was to write about contemporary Iberian and Latin American affairs, but in no time at all the lands south of the Rio Grande took over, inspiring journeys to all corners of the subcontinent. Ben has contributed to newspapers, magazines and learned tomes, usually on the subject of travel, and became editor of the *South American Handbook* in 1989. He has also been involved in Footprint's Handbooks on *Central America & Mexico, Caribbean Islands, Brazil, Peru, Cuzco & the Inca Heartland, Bolivia, Peru, Bolivia and Ecuador* and *Jamaica*. On many of these titles he has collaborated with his wife and Footprint Caribbean expert, Sarah Cameron.

Having a doctorate in Spanish and Portuguese studies from London University, Ben maintains a strong interest in Latin American literature. In the British summer he plays cricket for his local village side and year round he attempts to achieve some level of self-sufficiency in fruit and veg in a rather unruly country garden in Suffolk.

Acknowledgements

In September/October 2016 the author travelled from Brazil to Guyane, Suriname and Guyana and, for their assistance, hospitality and generosity, he would like to thank most warmly the following people:

In Guyana Tony Thorne and Claire Antell of Wilderness Explorers, plus the staff who helped organize the trip to Suriname and Guyana: Teri O'Brien, Kenneth Shivdyal, Amarylis Lewis, Annie Sonaram, and Ameer; and last but not least the tour guide Wally Prince. At Surama, Jackie Allicott and the staff and Kenneth Butler of Green Diamond Nature Tours. Rudy Edwards and the staff and community at Rewa. The staff at Atta, including Jonathan the guide, who found the screaming piha. At Karanambu, Melanie and Jerry McTurk and staff. Colin Edwards and family at Rock View. At Caiman House, Peter Taylor, Fernando, Josie, Jenkins and the rest of the staff. Finally, thanks to the tour members Isak, Maddy, Naila, Diana, Federika and Paul, who were such great travelling companions.

In Suriname Jerry A-Kum, Director of the Suriname Tourism Foundation; Dave Boucke, General Manager, Torarica, and member of SHATA; Robbin Roemer of 't Vat and Country Manager for Europcar; Sirano Zalman of Access Suriname Travel and Frederiksdorp, Tessa Leuwsha, Henk Tjassing, Tony the guide and the staff at Frederiksdorp.

In Guyane Laurence Besançon, Chargée de l'Observation et de la gestion du Système d'Informations Touristiques, and Rolando at the Comité du Tourisme de la Guyane in Cayenne.

We are grateful to Tessa Leuwsha for the survey of Surinamese literature and to Alex Robinson for the music section.

Ben would also like to thank the Footprint team who helped to put this edition together: Emma Bryers, Angus Dawson, Kevin Feeney and Felicity Laughton.

Credits

Footprint credits

Editor: Felicity Laughton
Production and layout: Emma Bryers
Maps: Kevin Feeney
Colour section: Angus Dawson

Publisher: John Sadler
Head of Publishing: Felicity Laughton
Marketing: Kirsty Holmes
Advertising and Partnerships:
Debbie Wylde

Photography credits
Front cover: Erik Zandboer/
Shutterstock.com
Back cover top: Anton_Ivanov/
Shutterstock.com
Back cover bottom: Mirko Rosenau/
Shutterstock.com
Inside front cover: Anna Jedynak/
Shutterstock.com

Colour section
Page 1: amskad/Shutterstock.com
Page 2: Pete Oxford/Superstock.com
Page 4: Natalia Gornyakova/
Shutterstock.com, Gail Johnson/
Shutterstock.com
Page 5: Matyas Rehak/Shutterstock.com,
Arjen de Ruiter/Shutterstock.com
Page 6: robertharding/Superstock.com
Page 7: Matyas Rehak/Shutterstock.com,
amskad/Shutterstock.com
Page 8: Rene Holtslag/Shutterstock.com

Duotone
Page 24: Matyas Rehak/Shutterstock.com.

Printed in India by Replika Press Pvt Ltd

Publishing information
Footprint Guyana, Guyane & Suriname
2nd edition
© Footprint Handbooks Ltd
August 2017

ISBN: 978 1 911082 40 8
CIP DATA: A catalogue record for this
book is available from the British Library

® Footprint Handbooks and the
Footprint mark are a registered
trademark of Footprint Handbooks Ltd

Published by Footprint
5 Riverside Court
Lower Bristol Road
Bath BA2 3DZ, UK
T +44 (0)1225 469141
footprinttravelguides.com

Distributed in the USA by
National Book Network, Inc.

Every effort has been made to ensure
that the facts in this guidebook are
accurate. However, travellers should still
obtain advice from consulates, airlines,
etc about travel and visa requirements
before travelling. The authors and
publishers cannot accept responsibility
for any loss, injury or inconvenience
however caused.